From Zero to Eleven Plus: Mathematics
Self-tutor study guide for Upper Primary, Lower Secondary and High S

C000162685

From Zero to Eleven Plus: Mathematics covers a comprehensive range of mathematica
primary, lower secondary and Eleven Plus students. In five distinct sections, the student is
basic to high-level questions in section one, challenging Eleven Plus questions with explanation in section two, differentiated
one step to creative multi-step questions for consolidation in section three, scholarship-type questions in section four and
timed written tests for assessment and development in section five. Back-tracking tips are provided in section one and two,
under the acronym WIN, which stands for 'What I Need'. All sections are written with the aim of developing the student's
ability to think creatively and understand what maths is required and how to apply it to solve increasingly complex problems.

From Zero to Eleven Plus: Mathematics is written by experienced practitioners, who have an exemplary record for making
a positive difference to exam grades and to gaining a place at a top secondary school. For less than the cost of one hour's
tutoring, it supports outstanding achievement.

Contents

ISBN: 978-0-9568427-1-8
First Edition – March 2011
Copyright © 2011 by Caroline Brice
Published by Andrew Crisp
3 Godson Road, CR0 4LT, UK
Tel: +44 (0)20 8686 9796
Email: books@zerotoelevenplus.co.uk
Web: www.zerotoelevenplus.co.uk
Editors: Caroline Brice and Amy Brice

From Zero to Eleven Plus: English and *From Zero to Eleven Plus: Verbal Reasoning* are also available.
For more information, please visit **www.zerotoelevenplus.co.uk**

£14.99

The four operations, one-step to multi-step problems

Inverse (opposite) operations: × ÷ Also: + −

Now it is your turn to practise...

Question:	4 pens cost 24p. How much is each pen?
WIN:	times-tables
WIN:	× ÷ are **inverse** (opposite) operations 4 ÷ 6 × 6 24
Answer and explanation:	4 × 6p = 24p 24p ÷ 4 = **6p**

Question:	1) 3 pens cost 36p. How much is each pen?
Think about 'What I Need' (WIN) first	

Question:	4 pens cost 24p. How much are 5 pens?
WIN:	Multi-step problems require more operations
WIN:	Find the cost of *one pen* first
Answer and explanation:	24p ÷ 4 = 6p (the cost of one pen) 6p × 5 = **30p** = *the cost of five pens*

Question:	2) 3 pens cost 36p. How much are 4 pens?
WIN:	

Question:	4 pens cost 24p. How much change is there from £1.00 if 5 pens are bought?
WIN:	**Number bonds** to 100, for example: 100 = 90 + 10 100 = 30 + 70

WIN:	To subtract, you are finding the difference between 2 numbers and it is easier to add on like this:
	
	100 − 38 = 62
	        2 60
	38 ⌢ 40 ⌢ 100 = 62
	
	100 − 57 = 43
	        3 40
	57 ⌢ 60 ⌢ 100 = 43

Answer and explanation:	24p ÷ 4 = 6p (the cost of one pen) 6p × 5 = 30p = the cost of five pens £1.00 − 30p = **70p**

Question:	3) 3 pens cost 36p. How much change is there from £1.00 if 4 pens are bought?
WIN:	

Question:	The change from £5 after buying 4 rulers is £2.64. How much would 5 rulers cost?
WIN:	£2.64 + £2.36 = £5.00 £4 100p £4.00 + £1.00 = £5.00
WIN:	£2.36 is the cost of four rulers
WIN:	0.59 4)2.36 59p is the cost of one ruler
Answer and explanation:	5 rulers = 5 × 59p = 295p = **£2.95**

Question:	4) Change from £5 after buying 3 notebooks is £2.90. How much would 4 notebooks cost?
WIN:	

Long multiplication and problems

Question:	How much are 12 chocolate bars at 34p each?
WIN:	Long multiplication, for example, 12p × 34: = £4.08 In steps: ❶ 4 × 2 ❸ Put a zero ❺ '3' × '1' ❷ 4 × '1' ten ❹ '3' × 2 ❻ 48 + 360

Question:	5) How much are 12 chocolate bars at 18p each?
*Think about 'What **I** Need' (WIN)*	

Question:	Altogether, how much are 3 chocolate bars at 56p each and 2 lollies at £1.03 each?
WIN:	56 1.03 × 3 × 2 1.68 + 2.06 1
WIN:	With column addition, align same value digits. So, £1.68 + £2.06 = **£3.74** 1.68 + 2.06 3.74 1

Question:	6) Altogether, how much are 6 chocolate bars at £1.23 each and 6 lollies at 39p each?
WIN:	

Question:	Explain why the answer is wrong:
	15 × 12 30 15 45
WIN:	Method of long multiplication
Answer and explanation:	15 × 12 30 150 ← 180 *this is supposed to be 10 × 15 = 150, remember to put in the zero*

Question:	7) Explain why the answer is wrong:
WIN:	25 × 16 150 25 175

Question:	Nine people go to the cinema at a cost of £19.30. Adult tickets cost £2.90 and children's tickets cost £1.20. How many adults go?
Answer and explanation:	Logically estimate, for example: 6 × £2.90 + 3 × £1.20 would be too much. Try: 5 × £2.90 + 4 × £1.20 £2.90 1.20 × 5 × 4 14.50 + 4.80 = £19.30 So the answer is **5 adults**

Question:	8) Nine people go to the cinema at a cost of £16.80. Adult tickets cost £4.10 and childrens tickets cost 75p. How many adults go?
WIN:	

Division, factors and problems

Now it is your turn to practise...

Question:	If 8 drinks cost £7.36, how much is each drink?
WIN:	❶ Put in any remainders ❷ Put in the decimal point directly above the decimal point in the number being divided
Answer and explanation:	$$\begin{array}{r} \overset{❷}{}0.92 \\ 8\,\overline{\smash{)}\,7.{}^7\!3{}^1\!6} \\ ❶ \end{array} = \textbf{92p}$$

Question:	9) If 7 books cost £90.30, how much is each book?
Think about 'What I Need' (WIN) first	

Question:	If 30 drinks cost £7.20, how much is each drink?
WIN:	Use **factor pairs** of 30 to break the division sum down
WIN:	**Factors** are numbers that divide into a number with no remainder, for example: 30 has factors: 1, 2, 3, 5, 6, 10, 15, 30
WIN:	**Factor pairs** multiply to make the number. Factor pairs of 30 are: 1,30 2,15 3,10 5,6
WIN:	7.20 ÷ 30 = 7.20 ÷ 10 ÷ 3 *or* 7.20 ÷ 6 ÷ 5
Answer and explanation:	$$\begin{array}{r} 1.20 \\ 6\,\overline{\smash{)}\,7.{}^1\!2\,0} \end{array}$$ $$\begin{array}{r} 0.24 \\ 5\,\overline{\smash{)}\,1.{}^1\!2{}^2\!0} \end{array}$$ 7.20 ÷ 30 = **24p**

Question:	10) If 70 books cost £90.30, how much is each book?
WIN:	

Question:	Use the 'chunking' method to get the answer: 714 ÷ 34
WIN:	34 × 10 = 340 34 × 20 = 680
Answer and explanation:	$$\begin{array}{rl} 714 & \\ -680 & 34 \times 20 \\ \hline 34 & 34 \times 1 \end{array}$$ 714 ÷ 34 = **21**

Question:	11) Use chunking to get the answer: 736 ÷ 23
WIN:	

Question:	Write three division sums with answers that show that answers to division sums can depend on the context of the 'story'.
Answer and explanation:	For example: • 15 ÷ 10 = 1.5 • How many full bags of 10 cakes are made from 15 cakes? = **1** • If 15 cakes are cooked on trays that hold 10 cakes each, how many trays are needed? = **2**

Question:	12) *Explain why* when I divide 9 by 6 I get the answer 1.5 and yet when I ask: there are 9 eggs, how many egg boxes (each hold 6 eggs) do I need to transport the eggs, I get the answer 2?
WIN:	

Addition, subtraction and problems

Question:	If I buy an apple for 65p, a sandwich for £1.24 and a juice for 45p, how much do I spend altogether?
WIN:	Align the same value digits ❶ Carry over any 'tens' or 'hundreds'
Answer and explanation:	$\begin{array}{r} 1.24 \\ .65 \\ +\ .45 \\ \hline 2.34 \\ {}_{1}\ {}_{1} \end{array}$ = £2.34 ❶

Question:	13) If I buy a ball for £1.99 and a bat for £2.24, how much I do spend?
*Think about 'What **I** Need' (**WIN**) first*	

Question:	I have £3.58 and I spend £1.49, how much change do I have left?
WIN:	Align the same value digits ❶ If bottom heavy, then *borrow*
Answer and explanation:	❶ $\begin{array}{r} 3.\overset{4}{\cancel{5}}\overset{1}{8} \\ -\ 1.49 \\ \hline 2.09 \end{array}$ = £2.09

Question:	14) I have £2.50, I spend 89p, how much change do I have left?
WIN:	

Question:	Two burgers and one portion of chips cost £2.60. Two portions of chips cost £1.20. How much is one burger and one portion of chips?
WIN:	Start with what you know
Answer and explanation:	Two portions of chips cost £1.20 Therefore, one portion costs 60p So, two burgers cost: £2.60 – 60p = £2.00 Therefore, one burger costs £1.00 One burger and one portion of chips costs: £1.00 + 60p = **£1.60**

Question:	15) A pizza and two portions of chips cost £3.25. If the chips are 50p each, how much would 2 pizzas and 2 portions of chips cost?
WIN:	

Question:	A pie and two juices cost £3.80 Two pies and two juices cost £6.80 How much is one pie and one juice?
WIN:	Notice that the second price includes the cost of *one more* pie
Answer and explanation:	So a pie costs: £6.80 – £3.80 = £3.00 Two juices therefore cost 80p One juice costs 80p ÷ 2 = 40p One pie and one juice costs: £3.00 + 40p = **£3.40**

Question:	16) Two portions of chips and an egg cost £1.75. If four portions of chips and an egg cost £3.25, how much do two portions of chips and two eggs cost?
WIN:	

Multiplying/dividing by 10,100,1000, conversion, money and 10%

Place value, × ÷ by 10, 100, 1000, distance conversion

Question:	Write the rule for dividing by 100
WIN:	The decimal system works on numbers being worth: 10 times more in columns to the left, and 10 times less to the right. Place value: hundreds, tens, units • tenths, hundredths
WIN:	To multiply by 10, move the digit left 1 place T U　　　　T U 　 4　　　　4 0
WIN:	To divide by 100, move the digit right 2 places H T U　　H T U 4 0 0　　　　 4

Question:	Order these numbers (shortest to longest distance): 1,210m 1.2km 123,000cm 1,200,004mm
WIN:	mm = millimetres　cm = centimetres m = metres　　　　km = kilometres
WIN:	×10　　　　×100　　　　×1000 1cm = 10mm　1m = 100cm　1km = 1000m 　÷10　　　　÷100　　　　÷1000
Answer and explanation:	1.2km 1,200,004mm 1,210m 123,000cm

Question:	What is 1km – 1cm?
WIN:	Know 1km = 100,000cm
Answer and explanation:	100,000cm – 1cm = **99,999cm** or **0.99999km**

Question:	If a tortoise travels 30m every 45 minutes, what speed is it going and how far will it go in two hours?
WIN:	speed = $\dfrac{\text{distance}}{\text{time}}$
WIN:	1 hour = 60 minutes
Answer and explanation:	30 metres in 45 minutes = 10 metres in 15 minutes = 40 metres in 60 minutes (1 hour) **Speed = 40 metres per hour** **The tortoise will travel 80 metres in 2 hours**

Now it is your turn to practise...

Question:	1) Write the rule for dividing by 1000
Think about 'What I Need' (WIN) first	

Question:	Order these numbers (shortest to longest distance): 2) i) 0.19m 220mm 21cm ii) 0.7km 710m 7000m
WIN:	

Question:	3) What is 1km – 1mm?
WIN:	

Question:	4) If an alien takes an hour to walk 1.2 km walking half the speed of a human, how long will it take the human to walk 400m?
WIN:	

Weight conversion and imperial measurements

Question:	Mark on these scales 750g:
WIN:	1kg = 1000g
WIN:	³/₄ kg = 750g
WIN:	Find the value of each gap on a scale by dividing weight by number of gaps
Answer and explanation:	750g 0　↓　1kg 750g 0　↓　(1000g)

Question:	If an apple weighs 70g, what does it weigh in kilograms?
WIN:	To convert grams into kilograms, divide by 1000
WIN:	To convert kilograms into grams, multiply by 1000
Answer and explanation:	70g = **0.07kg**

Question:	Convert these measurements of ingredients for lemonade into metric measurements: **3.6 pints water** **3.3 lbs lemons** **0.22 lbs castor sugar**
WIN:	2.2 lbs = 1 kg (1000g) 1.8 pints = 1 litre (1000cl)
Answer and explanation:	1.8 pints = 1 litre 3.6 pints = **2 litres (2000 ml)** 2.2 lbs = 1 kg 3.3 lbs = **1.5 kg (1500g)** 2.2 lbs = 1 kg 0.22 lbs = **0.1 kg (100g)**

Question:	Use < = > between one stone and one kilogram to show which is heavier.
WIN:	1 stone ≈ 6.35 kg Greater than > less than equals = Less than < greater than
WIN:	2.2 lbs ≈ 1 kg 14 lbs = 1 stone 1 stone ≈ 6.35 kg
Answer and explanation:	**one stone > one kilogram** *(you need 6.35 kg to be equivalent to 1 stone)*

Now it is your turn to practise...

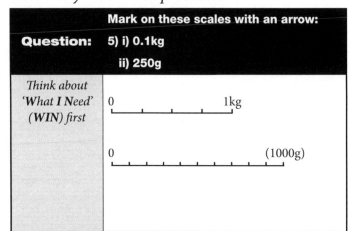

	Mark on these scales with an arrow:
Question:	5) i) 0.1kg ii) 250g
*Think about 'What I Need' (**WIN**) first*	0 ⊢——┴——┴——┴ 1kg 0 ⊢—┴—┴—┴—┴—┴—┴—┴—┴—┴ (1000g)

Question:	6) Find the weight of five objects, light to heavy, to get an idea of weight. Put the measurements in grams and kilograms.
WIN:	

Question:	7) Complete the conversion tables for imperial and metric units:
WIN:	(tables below)

inches (in)	1	2		40
centimetres (cm)	2.54		25.4	

kilograms (kg)	1	2		10
pounds (lbs)			11	

litres (litre)	1	2		40
pints	1.8		18	

Question:	8) Complete the conversion table below for stone/kg, and then work out your weight in stone and in kilograms.
WIN:	(table below)

Stone	1	2	3	4	5
Kg					

Capacity conversion

Question:	How can millilitres be converted to centilitres?
WIN:	If, one litre = 100 cl and one litre = 1000 ml, centilitres are 10 times bigger than millilitres So, 1 cl = 10 ml $\times 10$ cl $\rightleftarrows$ ml $\div 10$
Answer and explanation:	So, to convert ml to cl divide by 10 *(as you need less centilitres)*

Question:	Ann pours out 24 cl, then 345 ml of water from a litre bottle. How many millilitres are left?
WIN:	1 litre = 1000 ml 1 litre = 100 cl
Answer and explanation:	24 cl = 240 ml 240 ml + 345 ml = 585 ml 1 litre = 1000 ml 1000 ml − 585 ml = **415 ml**

Question:	A tap drips 2 ml of water per second. After ten minutes, how many litres of water has the tap dripped?
WIN:	60 seconds = 1 minute
Answer and explanation:	60 seconds = 1 minute 600 seconds = 10 minutes 600 × 2 ml = 1200 ml $\div 1000$ ml $\rightleftarrows$ litre $\times 1000$ 1200 ml ÷ 1000 = **1.2 litres**

Question:	Convert 65 cl out of a litre to the simplest fraction.
WIN:	1 litre = 100 cl So, $\dfrac{65 \text{ cl}}{100 \text{ cl}}$
WIN:	To convert to the simplest fraction divide both the top (numerator) and bottom (denominator) of the fraction by the highest number that can divide into them with no remainder
Answer and explanation:	$\div 5$ So, $\dfrac{65}{100}$ $\dfrac{13}{20}$ $\mathbf{\dfrac{13}{20}}$ $\div 5$

Now it is your turn to practise...

Question:	9) Complete this table:
Think about 'What I Need' (WIN) first	<table><tr><th>litre</th><th>cl</th><th>ml</th></tr><tr><td>2</td><td></td><td></td></tr><tr><td></td><td>350</td><td></td></tr><tr><td></td><td></td><td>4800</td></tr></table>

Question:	10) i) How many 125ml glasses of water can be poured from a 1 litre bottle.
WIN:	

Question:	11) A tap drips 3 ml of water per second. After quarter of an hour, how many litres of water has the tap dripped?
WIN:	

Question:	Convert these amounts out of a litre to the simplest fraction: 12) i) 500ml ii) 24cl iii) 350ml iv) 75cl
WIN:	

Money and 10%

Now it is your turn to practise...

Question:	What is £1.00 – 68p? Use a calculator to find £1.60 × 4
WIN:	Money works on the decimal system. So, £1.00 = 100p = 10 × 10p = 100 × 1p
WIN:	Know number bonds to 100 So, 68 + 32 = 100 90 + 10 = 100
WIN:	Money calculations on a calculator can leave out a zero if the decimal point is used after pounds. So, 0.4 = 40p 0.04 = 4p
Answer and explanation:	1.00 – 0.68 = 0.32 In money terms, 0.32 = **32p** 1.6 x 4 = 6.4 In money terms, 6.4 = **£6.40**

Question:	13) i) What is £1.00 – 83p? ii) Use a calculator to find £1.86 × 5
Think about 'What I Need' (WIN) first	

Question:	Find 10%, then 30% of: i) 60p ii) £6.00
WIN:	% means out of 100. So, 10% = $^{10}/_{100}$ = $^{1}/_{10}$
WIN:	To find 10% divide by 10 To find 30% (3×10%) divide by 10 and multiply by 3
Answer and explanation:	60p ÷ 10 = **6p** £6.00 = 600p ÷ 10 = **60p** 60p $\xrightarrow{÷ 10}$ 6p $\xrightarrow{× 3}$ **18p** £6.00 $\xrightarrow{÷ 10}$ 60p $\xrightarrow{× 3}$ **£1.80**

Question:	Find 10% of: 14) i) 70p ii) £7.00 Find 30% of: iii) 70p iv) £7.00
WIN:	

Question:	A tie costing £23 is reduced by 10%. What does it cost now?
WIN:	To find a 10% reduction: find 10% and take away from the whole cost.
Answer and explanation:	10% of £23 = £2.30 £23.00 – £2.30 = **£20.70**

Question:	15) A shirt costing £45 is reduced by 10%. What does it cost now?
WIN:	

Question:	A shirt now costs £16 after a 20% reduction. What did it cost?
WIN:	Understand that: 80% of the original cost = £16
Answer and explanation:	Know that: 80% = $^{8}/_{10}$ = £16 To find $^{1}/_{10}$ from $^{8}/_{10}$ divide by 8 = £2 | £2 | £2 | £2 | £2 | £2 | £2 | £2 | £2 | £2 | £2 | To find 100% ($^{10}/_{10}$) from $^{1}/_{10}$ multiply by 10 £2 × 10 = **£20**

Question:	16) A shirt now costs £45 after a 10% reduction. What did it cost?
WIN:	

Fractions, percentages and decimals

Finding a percentage of a number

Now it is your turn to practise...

Question:	Find: 5% of 80
WIN:	Factors of 100 are easy percentages to find with one division sum. For example: 25% = $1/4$ so divide by 4
Answer and explanation:	$5\% = {}^{5}/_{100} = {}^{1}/_{20}$ ${}^{1}/_{20}$ of 80 = **4**

Question:	Find: 1) i) 10% of 60 ii) 20% of 60 iii) 25% of 60 iv) 50% of 60
Think about 'What I Need' (WIN) first	

Question:	Find: 80% of 120
WIN:	To find some percentages, *two operations* are required. So to find 80%, that is $^{8}/_{10}$ divide by 10 to find 10% and multiply by 8.
Answer and explanation:	80% of 120: $(120 \div 10 = 12) \times 8 = \mathbf{96}$

Question:	Find: 2) i) 40% of 80 ii) 70% of 80 iii) 90% of 80 iv) 75% of 80
WIN:	

Question:	Find: 12% of 300
WIN:	Percentages that are not multiples of 10 or 5 can be found by finding 1%, that is $^{1}/_{100}$ and multiplying up.
Answer and explanation:	12% of 300: $(^{300}/_{100} = 3) \times 12 = \mathbf{36}$

Question:	Find: 3) i)1% of 200 ii) 3% of 200 iii) 57% of 200 iv) 94% of 200
WIN:	

Question:	Find: 150% of 80
WIN:	Know $150\% = {}^{150}/_{100} = {}^{15}/_{10}$ or 150% = 1.5
Answer and explanation:	$80 \times 1.5 = \mathbf{120}$

Question:	Find: 4) 200% of 80
WIN:	

Expressing percentages as division and multiplication sums using n (any number)

Question:	Write a formula using n (any number) to show how to find: i) 20% ii) 120%
WIN:	If n can be used to represent any number, then a formula can be written to show a maths system.
WIN:	Think what multiplication and/or division are required to get each answer
WIN:	10% ($1/10$) of any number is: $n \div 10$ or $n/10$ Example: $n = 90$ 10% of 90 = $90/10 = 9$
WIN:	Know 20% = $2 \times 10\%$ For example, 20% of 60 = ($60/10 = 6$) $\times 2 = 12$
Answer and explanation:	To find 20% of n $n/10 \times 2$ or $n/5$ To find 120%, know that 120% = $12/10$ So, $n/10 \times 12$

Question:	Use n to write a formula to find 3%
WIN:	1% = $1/100$ 3% = $3/100$ So, 3% is $3 \times 1\%$
Answer and explanation:	Know to find 1%, then multiply by 3 So, $n/100 \times 3$

Question:	Give two examples of formulae to find 70% of n
WIN:	Know 70% = $70/100 = 70 \times 1/100$ Know $70/100 = 7/10 = 7 \times 1/10$
Answer and explanation:	So, $n/100 \times 70$ or $n/10 \times 7$

Question:	Use a calculator to find 34% of: i) 150 ii) 200 iii) 400
WIN:	Know 34% = $34/100 = 0.34$
Answer and explanation:	To find 34% of 150 enter: $0.34 \times 150 = \mathbf{51}$ 34% of 200, enter: 34% of 200 = $0.34 \times 200 = \mathbf{68}$ 34% of 400, enter: 34% of 400 = $0.34 \times 400 = \mathbf{136}$

Now it is your turn to practise...

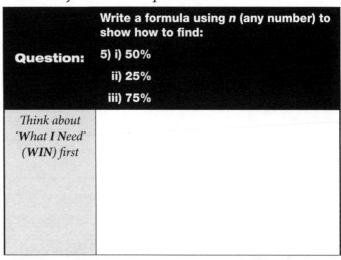

Question:	Write a formula using n (any number) to show how to find: 5) i) 50% ii) 25% iii) 75%
Think about 'What I Need' (WIN) first	

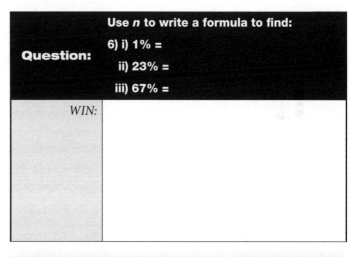

Question:	Use n to write a formula to find: 6) i) 1% = ii) 23% = iii) 67% =
WIN:	

Question:	7) i) Write two different formulae, using n to show how to find 5% of n? ii) How could you find 15% of n?
WIN:	

Question:	Use a calculator to find 72% of: 8) i) 200 ii) 900
WIN:	

Equivalent values of fractions, decimals and percentages, greater/less than, fraction sums

Question:	Convert $^9/_{20}$, $^4/_5$ and $^1/_2$ to percentages and decimals
WIN:	% is out of 100
Answer and explanation:	$\times 5$ So, $^9/_{20} = {^{45}}/_{100} = \textbf{45\%} = \textbf{0.45}$ $\times 5$ $0.45 = 45\%$ $^4/_{10} = {^{40}}/_{100} + {^5}/_{100}$ $\times 20$ So, $^4/_5 = {^{80}}/_{100} = \textbf{80\%} = \textbf{0.8}$ $\times 20$ $\times 50$ So, $^1/_2 = {^{50}}/_{100} = \textbf{50\%} = \textbf{0.5}$ $\times 50$

Question:	Insert > < or = between: $^1/_6$ 17%
WIN:	less than < greater than > For example: 2 < 4 and 4 > 2
WIN:	Know to turn $^1/_6$ into a decimal, divide 1 by 6
Answer and explanation:	$\begin{array}{r} 0.16\dot{6} \\ 6\overline{|1.0^{1}0^{4}0^{4}} \end{array}$ $0.166 = 16.6\%$ So, $^1/_6 < \textbf{17\%}$

Question:	Find: i) $^1/_2 + ^1/_3 =$ ii) $^1/_2 - ^1/_3 =$ iii) $^1/_2 \times ^1/_3 =$ iv) $^1/_2 \div ^1/_3 =$
WIN:	**Equivalent fractions** can be added and subtracted. So, $^1/_2 + ^1/_3$ $^1/_2 - ^1/_3$ $\times 3$ $\times 2$ $\times 3$ $\times 2$ $^3/_6 + ^2/_6 = \textbf{}^5/_6$ $^3/_6 - ^2/_6 = \textbf{}^1/_6$
WIN:	**Multiply** fractions by multiplying: **top × top** (numerators) **bottom × bottom** (denominators) 1×1 $^1/_2 \times ^1/_3 = \textbf{}^1/_6$ 2×3
WIN:	**Divide** fractions by turning second fraction upside down and then multiplying numerators and denominators. $^1/_2 \div ^1/_3 = ^1/_2 \times ^3/_1 = ^3/_2 = 1^1/_2 = 1.5$
Answer and explanation:	i) $^5/_6$ ii) $^1/_6$ iii) $^1/_6$ iv) $1^1/_2$ or **1.5**

Now it is your turn to practise...

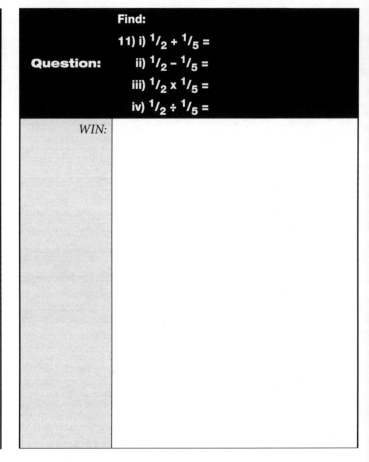

Question:	9) Complete this table:

Think about 'What I Need' (WIN) first	**Fraction**	**%**	**Decimal**
	9i) $^1/_{10} = {^{10}}/_{100}$		
	9ii)		0.5
	9iii)	25%	
	9iv) $^3/_4$		
	9v)		0.01
	9vi) $^2/_5$		

Question:	Use: > < = 10) i) $^1/_8$ 0.12 ii) $^1/_7$ 0.14 iii) 0.11 11%
WIN:	

Question:	Find: 11) i) $^1/_2 + ^1/_5 =$ ii) $^1/_2 - ^1/_5 =$ iii) $^1/_2 \times ^1/_5 =$ iv) $^1/_2 \div ^1/_5 =$
WIN:	

Improper fractions, division, finding a fraction of an amount and an amount of a fraction

Now it is your turn to practise...

Question:	Find: $^3/_2 =$
WIN:	Improper fractions are top heavy fractions, for example: $^3/_2 =$ 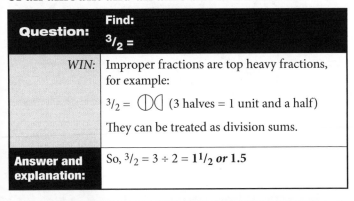 (3 halves = 1 unit and a half) They can be treated as division sums.
Answer and explanation:	So, $^3/_2 = 3 \div 2 = 1^1/_2$ *or* **1.5**

Question:	Find: $^3/_5$ of 10
WIN:	If you are finding a fifth, divide by 5 $^1/_5$ of 10 = 2 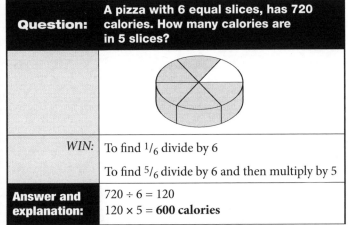
WIN:	Find $^3/_5$ of 10 by dividing by 5 and multiplying by 3
Answer and explanation:	$^3/_5$ of 10 = **6**

Question:	A pizza with 6 equal slices, has 720 calories. How many calories are in 5 slices?
	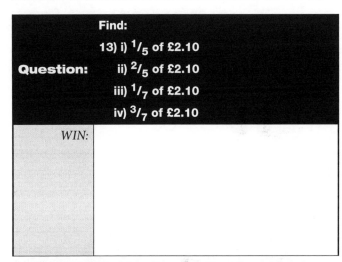
WIN:	To find $^1/_6$ divide by 6 To find $^5/_6$ divide by 6 and then multiply by 5
Answer and explanation:	$720 \div 6 = 120$ $120 \times 5 = $ **600 calories**

Question:	Sade gets a score of 150 which is $^3/_4$ of the test marks. What is the test out of?
WIN:	$^3/_4 = 150$ 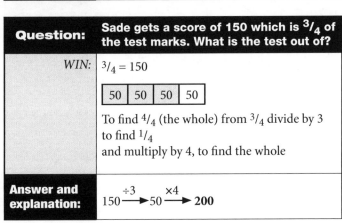 To find $^4/_4$ (the whole) from $^3/_4$ divide by 3 to find $^1/_4$ and multiply by 4, to find the whole
Answer and explanation:	$150 \xrightarrow{\div 3} 50 \xrightarrow{\times 4}$ **200**

Question:	Find: 12) i) $^{20}/_5 =$ ii) $^{22}/_3 =$ iii) $^{21}/_3 =$ iv) $^{26}/_4 =$
Think about 'What I Need' (WIN) first	

Question:	Find: 13) i) $^1/_5$ of £2.10 ii) $^2/_5$ of £2.10 iii) $^1/_7$ of £2.10 iv) $^3/_7$ of £2.10
WIN:	

Question:	14) A cake with 8 equal slices, has 720 calories. How many calories are in 5 slices?
WIN:	

Question:	15) Tom gets a score of 120 which is $^4/_5$ of the test marks. What is the test out of?
WIN:	

Fractions, probability, ratio and proportion

Fractions and ratio

Now it is your turn to practise...

Question: Shade in squares with the ratio 2:3 (shaded to unshaded)

i)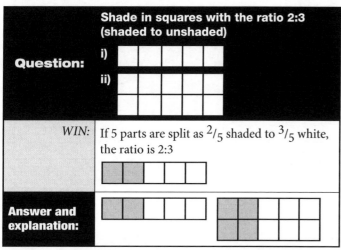
ii)

WIN: If 5 parts are split as $^2/_5$ shaded to $^3/_5$ white, the ratio is 2:3

Answer and explanation:

Question: Shade in squares with the ratio 1:2 (shaded to unshaded)

1) i)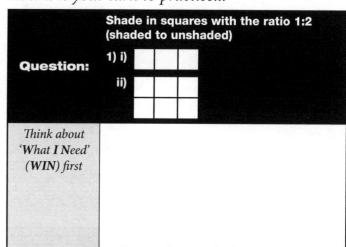
ii)

Think about 'What I Need' (WIN) first

Question: What is the ratio of shaded to unshaded squares (simplest terms):

WIN:

2:4
shaded   unshaded

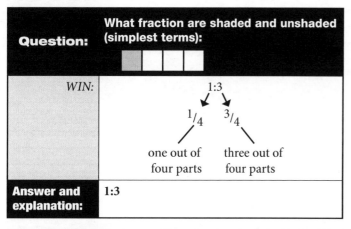

Answer and explanation: 2:4 can be simplified as both can be divided by 2.

So, 2:4 = **1:2**

Question: What is the ratio of shaded to unshaded shares (simplest terms):

2) i)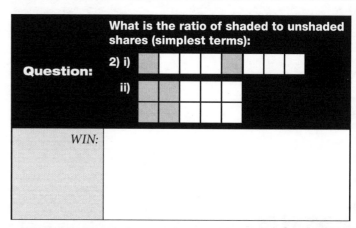
ii)

WIN:

Question: What fraction are shaded and unshaded (simplest terms):

WIN:

1:3

$^1/_4$ $^3/_4$

one out of   three out of
four parts   four parts

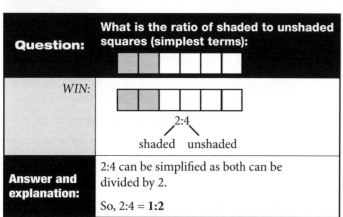

Answer and explanation: 1:3

Question: What fraction are shaded and unshaded (simplest terms):

3) i)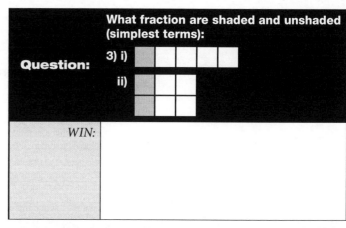
ii)

WIN:

Question: Shade in $^1/_3$ of the triangles and write the ratio for shaded : unshaded triangles

WIN:

Know there are 12 equal parts

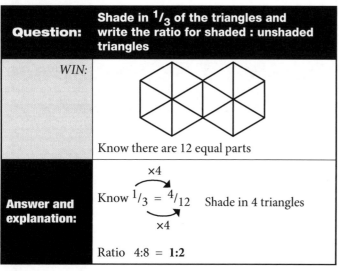

Answer and explanation:

Know $^1/_3 = {}^4/_{12}$ Shade in 4 triangles
×4 ×4

Ratio 4:8 = **1:2**

Question: 4) i) Shade in $^1/_6$ of the triangles, and
ii) write the ratio for shaded : unshaded triangles

WIN:

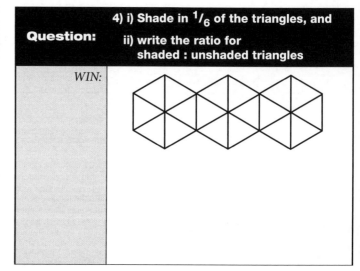

Ratio and probability

Question:	What is the probability of rolling an even number on a normal die? Express this as a ratio for even to odd numbers.
WIN:	Probability is easily expressed as a fraction. For example, on a normal die there is $3/6$ probability of rolling an even number because there are three out of six even numbers.
Answer and explanation:	Simplify to: $\div 3$ **Probability of** $3/6 \quad 1/2$ **rolling an even** $\div 3$ **number** $= 1/2$ Ratio of even (even) **1 : 1** (odd) to odd numbers $\downarrow$ $\downarrow$ (1/2 1/2)

Question:	5) i) On a normal die what is the probability (simplest form) of rolling a number less than three? ii) Express the ratio of numbers less than 3 : numbers greater than 3
Think about 'What I Need' (WIN) first	

Question:	Balls are placed in a bag in the ratio 2:5 black to white. i) If there are 6 black balls, how many white balls are there? ii) What is the probability of picking a black ball?
WIN:	Operations used in ratio and proportion are mainly: $\times \div$

Answer and explanation:	$\times 3 \begin{pmatrix} 2:5 \\ 6:15 \end{pmatrix} \times 3$
	
	 6 black balls : **15 white balls**
	       2 : 5
	     $\downarrow$ $\downarrow$
	    $2/7$ $5/7$
	 Probability of picking a black ball = $2/7$

Question:	Balls are placed in a bag in the ratio 2:3 black to white. 6) i) If there are 8 black balls, how many white balls are there? ii) What is the probability of picking a black ball?
WIN:	

Question:	Black to white balls are in a bag in the ratio 1:2 (three balls in total). If a white ball is taken out, what is the new ratio and probability of picking a black ball?
WIN:	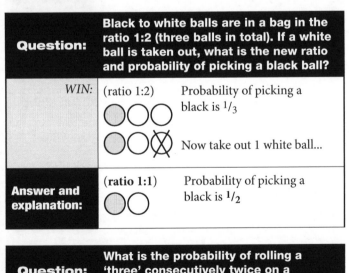
Answer and explanation:	

Question:	7) Green to red balls are in the ratio 1:7 (eight balls in total). If a red ball is taken out, what is the ratio now for green to red balls? And, what is the new probability of choosing a red ball?
WIN:	

Question:	What is the probability of rolling a 'three' consecutively twice on a normal die?
WIN:	The probability of rolling a '3' on a normal die is $1/6$. The probability of rolling a 3 twice is $1/6 \times 1/6$

Answer and explanation:	Multiply fractions by multiplying:
	     top $\times$ top (numerators)
	 bottom $\times$ bottom (denominators)
	     $1/6 \times 1/6 = 1/36$

Question:	8) What is the probability of throwing a 'head' consecutively twice on a coin?
WIN:	

Ratio of amounts

Now it is your turn to practise...

Question:	Split £18 in the ratio 2:7
WIN:	Splitting an amount using ratio is easily done through counting up parts to find the fraction, for example: 2:7 = 2 + 7 = 9 parts $\quad\quad\quad\quad$ $2/_9$ $\quad$ $7/_9$
Answer and explanation:	2:7 $2/_9$ $\quad$ $7/_9$ $\quad$ of £18 **£4** $\quad$ **£14**

Question:	Money is split in the ratio 2:3. How much would each person get if splitting: 9) i) £10 $\quad$ ii) £40 $\quad$ iii) £35
Think about 'What I Need' (WIN) first	

Question:	In a class the ratio of (Boys) 3: 2 (Girls) i) If there are 25 children in the class, how many are girls? ii) If there are 12 girls in the class, how many children are there in total?
WIN:	Boys : Girls $3/_5$ $\quad$ $2/_5$
WIN:	Boys : Girls $\quad\quad$ 3 : 2 ×6 $\quad\quad\quad$ ×6 $\quad\quad$ 18 : 12
Answer and explanation:	i) $2/_5$ of 25 = **10** ii) 18 + 12 = **30**

Question:	On a school trip the ratio of: Adults : Boys : Girls $\quad$ 1 : 5 : 6 10) i) If 72 people go on the trip, how many are boys? $\quad\quad$ ii) If there are 55 boys on the trip, how many people are there in total?
WIN:	

Question:	In a class the ratio of (Boys) 3: 2 (Girls) If there are 8 more boys than girls, how many boys and girls are there in total?
WIN:	3:2 $\quad\quad$ Go up in proportional steps to 6:4 $\quad\quad$ find the difference of 8 9:6 12:8 15:10 $\quad\quad$ or note that the difference of 18:12 $\quad\quad$ boys to girls = 8 21:14 $\quad\quad$ with a ratio difference of 1 **24:16** $\quad\quad$ 8 ÷ 1 = 8 (steps) So, $\quad$ ×8 $\binom{3:2}{}$ ×8 $\quad\quad\quad\quad$ 24 : 16
Answer and explanation:	24 + 16 = **40**

Question:	On a school trip the ratio of: Adults : Boys : Girls $\quad$ 1 : 5 : 6 11) If there are 7 more girls than boys on the trip, how many boys are on the trip?
WIN:	

Question:	x is worth $3/_4$ of y What is the ratio of x to y ? If £28 is shared out, how much does x get and y get?
WIN:	$\quad\quad$ $x:y$ $\quad\quad$ 3:4 $\quad$ $3/_7$ $\quad$ $4/_7$
Answer and explanation:	$x : y$ $3/_7$ $\quad$ $4/_7$ $\quad$ $1/_7$ of £28 = 4 x = $3/_7$ = 3 × £4 = **£12** y = $4/_7$ = 4 × £4 = **£16**

Question:	x is worth 5 times as much as y and 2 times as much as z. 12) i) What is the ratio of x:y:z ? $\quad\quad$ ii) If £34 is shared by x, y, z how much more does x get than z ?
WIN:	

Ratio problems with conversion, data handling and algebra

Question:	Grey paint is made in the ratio: 5(white):2(blue):1(black)
	How many ml of white paint is needed to make 1 litre of grey paint?
WIN:	1 litre = 1000ml
Answer and explanation:	white = $^5/_8$ of 1 litre $^1/_8$ of 1000ml = $^{1000}/_8$ = 125ml 125ml × 5 = **625ml**

Question:	How many km is it from Cramwell to Dunderton if miles:km is 5:8 ?
	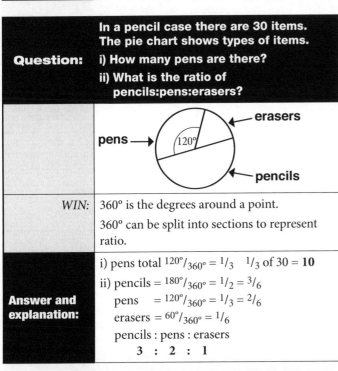
WIN:	Cramwell to Dunderton = 14 + 16 = 30 miles
Answer and explanation:	miles:km ×6 $\Big($ 5:8 $\Big)$ ×6 30 miles = **48km** 30:48

Question:	In a pencil case there are 30 items. The pie chart shows types of items. i) How many pens are there? ii) What is the ratio of pencils:pens:erasers?
	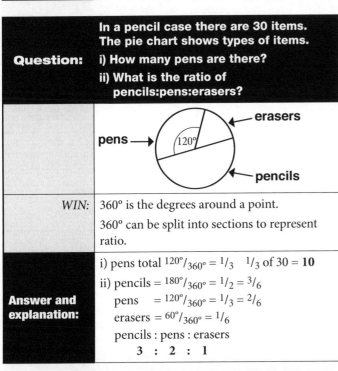
WIN:	360° is the degrees around a point. 360° can be split into sections to represent ratio.

Answer and explanation:	i) pens total $^{120°}/_{360°}$ = $^1/_3$ $^1/_3$ of 30 = **10**
	ii) pencils = $^{180°}/_{360°}$ = $^1/_2$ = $^3/_6$
	    pens = $^{120°}/_{360°}$ = $^1/_3$ = $^2/_6$
	    erasers = $^{60°}/_{360°}$ = $^1/_6$
	    pencils : pens : erasers
	       3 : 2 : 1

Question:	Frozen vegetables are mixed peas:sweetcorn (in weight) 3:1 How heavy is the packet if there are 600g of peas?

WIN:	Share out by converting to fractions.
	For example: peas:sweetcorn
	               3:1
	           $^3/_4$ $^1/_4$ $^3/_4$ = 600g

Answer and explanation:	$^1/_4$ = 600g ÷ 3 = 200g $^4/_4$ = 200g × 4 = **800g**

Now it is your turn to practise...

Question:	Orange paint is made in the ratio red to yellow 3:7
	13) How many ml of red paint are needed to make 1 litre of orange paint?
*Think about 'What I Need' (**WIN**) first*	

Question:	14) How many km is it from Ashertown to Botown if miles:km is 5:8 ?
WIN:	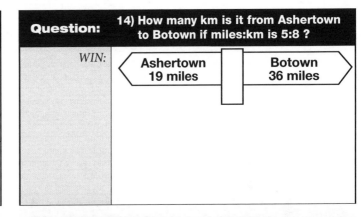

Question:	In a village there are 90 buildings. The pie chart shows types of buildings. 15) i) How many houses are in the village? ii) How many degrees represent the houses?
WIN:	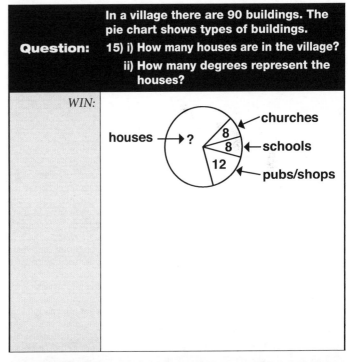

Question:	Peanuts to raisins (in weight) are mixed in the ratio 2:1 respectively. 16 i) How heavy is a packet wth 240g of peanuts? ii) If 240g mix costs 50p, how much would 360g cost?
WIN:	

Equations, sequences, finding rules and formulae

Equations – finding numerical values for letters

Now it is your turn to practise...

Question:	If $3a = 21$ What is $2a$?
WIN:	A letter can be used to represent a number So, if $a = 7$ $\qquad 2 \times a = 2a = 14$
Answer and explanation:	$3a = 21$ $3 \times a = 21$ $3 \times 7 = 21$ So, $a = 7$ $2a = 2 \times 7 = \mathbf{14}$

Question:	Find the value of each letter: 1) i) $x + 4 = 10$ $x = ?$ ii) $y - 8 = 12$ $y = ?$ iii) $3z = 21$ $5z = ?$
Think about 'What I Need' (WIN) first	

Question:	Find the value of x, when $\frac{2x}{3} = 12$
WIN:	Equations can involve several operations
Answer and explanation:	Find the value of $2x$ before dividing by 2 to find x $\frac{36}{3} = 12$ So, $2x = 36$ $\qquad x = \mathbf{18}$

Question:	Find the value of each letter: 2) i) $2x + 4 = 10$ $x = ?$ ii) $2y - 8 = 12$ $y = ?$ iii) $4z = 28$ $5z = ?$
WIN:	

Question:	If the perimeter = 40cm, what is the value of n?
	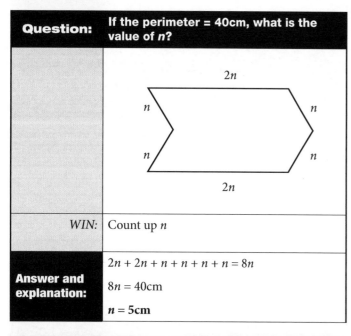
WIN:	Count up n
Answer and explanation:	$2n + 2n + n + n + n + n = 8n$ $8n = 40$cm $n = \mathbf{5cm}$

Question:	3) If the perimeter = 77cm, what is n worth?
WIN:	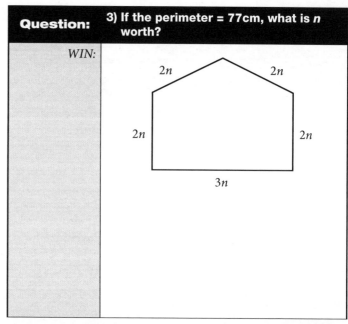

Question:	In a cutlery box there are n dessert spoons and twice as many knives as dessert spoons. There are twice as many forks as knives and 3 teaspoons. Altogether there are 38 items. How many forks are there?
WIN:	Count up the n + numbers
Answer and explanation:	$n + 2n + 4n + 3 = 7n + 3 = 38$ $7n = 35$ $\quad n = 5$ forks $= 4n = \mathbf{20}$

Question:	4) In a garden there are n pansies. There are twice as many daffodils and 4 roses. Altogether there are 34 flowers. What is n worth?
WIN:	

Sequences

Now it is your turn to practise...

Question:	Continue this sequence: 3, 6, 9, 12, _____
WIN:	The **rule** for simple sequences can usually be found by working out the difference between consecutive numbers (numbers next to each other), for example 3: +3 +3 +3 3, 6, 9, 12
WIN:	Sequences that go up exponentially (rapid increase) may involve indices (such as squared or cubed numbers), for example: Squared numbers: 1, 4, 9, 16, 25 Cubed numbers: 1, 8, 27, 64, 125
Answer and explanation:	3, 6, 9, 12, **15**

Question:	Is -4 in this sequence: 85, 81, 77, 73, 69 ?
WIN:	Sequences can be used to test other knowledge, such as negative numbers, fractions and times-tables.
WIN:	Note the difference between each consecutive number is 4
Answer and explanation:	$85 \div 4 = 21$ *remainder* 1 $4 \times 21 = 84$ $85 - 84 = 1$ $1 - 4 = -3$ so, **-4 is not in the sequence**

Question:	What is the next number in this sequence?
WIN:	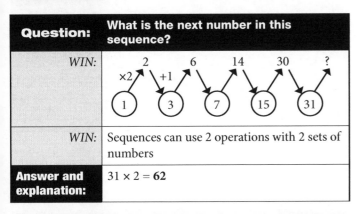
WIN:	Sequences can use 2 operations with 2 sets of numbers
Answer and explanation:	$31 \times 2 = \mathbf{62}$

Question:	Continue the sequence:
WIN:	Sequences can involve visual patterns with a corresponding sequence of numbers
Answer and explanation:	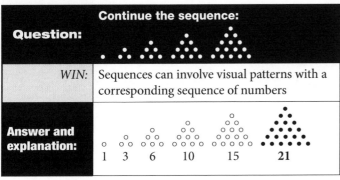

Question:	Continue these sequences: 5) i) 2, 4, 6, 8, _____, _____ ii) 10, 20, 30, _____, _____
Think about 'What I Need' (WIN) first	

Question:	Continue these sequences: 6) i) 5, 1, -3, -7, _____, _____ ii) 2, 1, $^1/_2$, $^1/_4$, _____, _____ iii) 99, 96, 93, 90 Explain why 3 is in this sequence.
WIN:	

Question:	7) Continue: 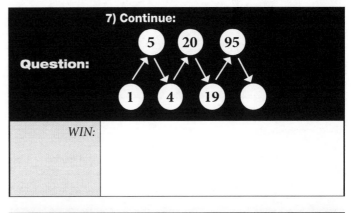
WIN:	

Question:	8) Write the next 5 numbers for this sequence: 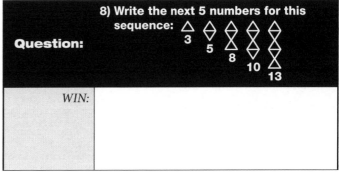
WIN:	

Rules and formulae using the nth term

Now it is your turn to practise...

Question:	Find the rule that connects n to the resultant number: n n n n $1 \rightarrow 4$ $2 \rightarrow 8$ $3 \rightarrow 12$ $4 \rightarrow 16$
WIN:	Find the same connection (rule) that links each n to its resultant number.
Answer and explanation:	Rule = × **4**

Question:	9) Find the rule and write the formula for: n n n n $1 \rightarrow 4$ $2 \rightarrow 8$ $3 \rightarrow 12$ $4 \rightarrow 16$
Think about 'What I Need' (WIN) first	

Question:	Find the rule that connects n to the resultant number and write a formula using n: n n n n $1 \rightarrow 2$ $2 \rightarrow 4$ $3 \rightarrow 6$ $4 \rightarrow 8$
WIN:	If a common rule links all n to their resultant numbers, a formula can be written using n (the nth term)
Answer and explanation:	In this case n $1 \rightarrow 2$ $2 \rightarrow 4$ $3 \rightarrow 6$ $4 \rightarrow 8$ × 2 $n \times 2 = 2n$

Question:	10) Find the rule that connects n to the resultant number and write a formula using n: n n n n $1 \rightarrow 5$ $2 \rightarrow 10$ $3 \rightarrow 15$ $4 \rightarrow 20$
WIN:	

Question:	Find the rule that connects n to the resultant number, write a formula and use this to find the missing number: n $1 \rightarrow 2$ $2 \rightarrow 5$? $\rightarrow 44$ $3 \rightarrow 8$ $4 \rightarrow 11$
WIN:	Rules can involve two operations

Answer and explanation:	Find the difference between the resultant numbers
	
	2 5 8 11
	  3 3 3
	
	The difference will indicate how many n are involved, in this case $3n$
	
	Then the other operation is easy to see:
	   ×3 −1
	$1 \rightarrow 3 \rightarrow 2$
	$2 \rightarrow 6 \rightarrow 5$
	$3 \rightarrow 9 \rightarrow 8$
	$4 \rightarrow 12 \rightarrow 11$ So, **$3n-1$**
	
	Use inverse to find the missing number
	? $\rightarrow 44$
	
	$44 + 1 = 45 \div 3 = $ **15**

Question:	11) Find the rule that connects n to the resultant number, write a formula and use this to find the missing number: n $1 \rightarrow 3$ $2 \rightarrow 5$ $3 \rightarrow 7$ $4 \rightarrow 9$? $\rightarrow 21$
WIN:	

Use formulae to find amounts

Now it is your turn to practise...

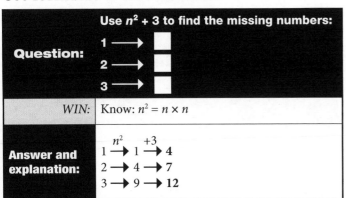

	Use $n^2 + 3$ to find the missing numbers:
Question:	1 ⟶ ☐ 2 ⟶ ☐ 3 ⟶ ☐
WIN:	Know: $n^2 = n \times n$
Answer and explanation:	$\begin{array}{ccc} & n^2 & +3 \\ 1 & \to 1 & \to \mathbf{4} \\ 2 & \to 4 & \to \mathbf{7} \\ 3 & \to 9 & \to \mathbf{12} \end{array}$

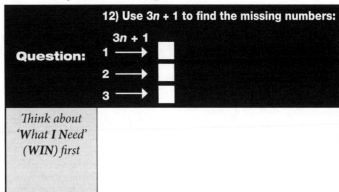

	12) Use $3n + 1$ to find the missing numbers:
Question:	$3n + 1$ 1 ⟶ ☐ 2 ⟶ ☐ 3 ⟶ ☐
*Think about 'What **I** Need' (**WIN**) first*	

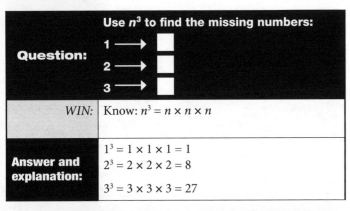

	Use n^3 to find the missing numbers:
Question:	1 ⟶ ☐ 2 ⟶ ☐ 3 ⟶ ☐
WIN:	Know: $n^3 = n \times n \times n$
Answer and explanation:	$1^3 = 1 \times 1 \times 1 = 1$ $2^3 = 2 \times 2 \times 2 = 8$ $3^3 = 3 \times 3 \times 3 = 27$

	13) Use $n^3 + 1$ to find the missing numbers:
Question:	$n^3 + 1$ 1 ⟶ ☐ 2 ⟶ ☐ 3 ⟶ ☐ ☐ ⟶ 1001
WIN:	

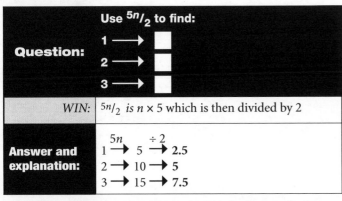

	Use $\frac{5n}{2}$ to find:
Question:	1 ⟶ ☐ 2 ⟶ ☐ 3 ⟶ ☐
WIN:	$\frac{5n}{2}$ is $n \times 5$ which is then divided by 2
Answer and explanation:	$\begin{array}{ccc} & 5n & \div 2 \\ 1 & \to 5 & \to \mathbf{2.5} \\ 2 & \to 10 & \to \mathbf{5} \\ 3 & \to 15 & \to \mathbf{7.5} \end{array}$

	14) Use $\frac{n}{10} \div 2$ to find:
Question:	20 ⟶ ☐ 30 ⟶ ☐ 40 ⟶ ☐
WIN:	

	Is there a simpler way to express the connection:
Question:	1 ⟶ 2.5 2 ⟶ 5 3 ⟶ 7.5
WIN:	$\frac{5n}{2}$ = divide the top and bottom by 2
Answer and explanation:	$\mathbf{2.5}n$

Question:	15) Is there a simpler way to express $\frac{n}{10} \div 2$?
WIN:	

Negative numbers, co-ordinates and translation

Negative integers and sums

Now it is your turn to practise...

Question:

Find the missing number:

$-1 +$ [?] $= 0$

WIN:

Integers are whole numbers.

Negative one is one less than zero.

Negative two is two less than zero, and worth one less than negative one.

$$-5\ -4\ -3\ -2\ -1\ \ 0\ \ 1\ \ 2\ \ 3\ \ 4\ \ 5$$

Answer and explanation:

Negative numbers can be seen as 'debt'. Adding a positive number takes away from debt.

So: $-2 + 1 = -1$

$-1 + \mathbf{1} = 0$

---

1) Find:

$-4 + 1 =$ [?]

$-4 + 2 =$ [?]

$-4 + 3 =$ [?]

$-4 + 4 =$ [?]

$-4 + 5 =$ [?]

Question:

Think about 'What I Need' (WIN) first

Question:

Find the missing number:

$-4 - -6 =$ [?]

WIN:

Subtracting a negative number takes away 'debt' and hence adds.

Two negatives make a positive.

Answer and explanation:

$-4 - -6 = \mathbf{2}$

---

2) Find:

$-4 - -1 =$ [?]

$3 - -1 =$ [?]

$6 - -2 =$ [?]

$8 - -5 =$ [?]

Question:

WIN:

Question:

Find:

$-7 + -3 =$ [?]

$-7 - -3 =$ [?]

$-7 + 3 =$ [?]

$-7 - 3 =$ [?]

WIN:

Add 'debt' by adding a negative number and so subtract.

Answer and explanation:

$-7 + -3 = \mathbf{-10}$

$-7 - -3 = \mathbf{-4}$

$-7 + 3 = \mathbf{-4}$

$-7 - 3 = \mathbf{-10}$

---

3) Find:

$-4 + -1 =$ [?]

$-4 + 1 =$ [?]

$-4 - 1 =$ [?]

$-4 - -1 =$ [?]

Question:

WIN:

Question:

Find the missing numbers:

$-5 +$ [?] $= 0$

$-5 +$ [?] $= -10$

$-5 -$ [?] $= 0$

$-5 -$ [?] $= -10$

WIN:

Remember:

• 2 negatives make a positive as you are taking away 'debt'

• adding a negative is *taking away*

Answer and explanation:

$-5 + \mathbf{5} = 0$

$-5 + \mathbf{-5} = -10$

$-5 - \mathbf{-5} = 0$

$-5 - \mathbf{5} = -10$

---

4) Find the missing numbers:

$-100 +$ [?] $= 0$

$-100 +$ [?] $= -200$

$-100 -$ [?] $= 0$

$-100 -$ [?] $= -200$

Question:

WIN:

Problems with negative numbers, using median, range

Question:	Outside a house the temperature is 20°C lower than inside the house. If it is -6°C outside the house, what is the temperature inside the house?
WIN:	Know how to add on from -6
Answer and explanation:	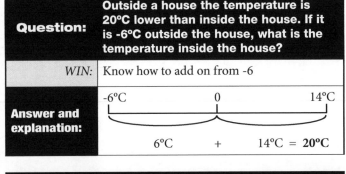

Question:	The temperature at night-time is -5°C and in the day-time it is 16°C, what is the difference between the temperatures?
WIN:	Find the **difference** by adding the negative number to zero 'gap' and the zero to positive number gap. 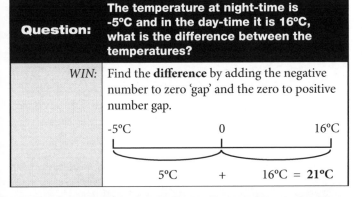

Question:	i) Put the numbers in order to find the median: 10, 12, -2, -4, 6 ii) What is the range of these numbers?
WIN:	**Median** is the middle number when the numbers are arranged in value order. For example: -1, 3, 7, 9, 10 Median = 7
WIN:	**Range** is the difference between the lowest and highest value numbers, for example: -1 and 10 = **11**
Answer and explanation:	i) write the numbers in value order: -4, -2, 6, 10, 12 Median = **6** ii) -4 and 12 = **16** Range = **16**

Question:	Temperature decreases at 2°C every 5 minutes. If the temperature starts at 4°C, what will the temperature be after an hour?
WIN:	An hour = 60 minutes
WIN:	There are 12 × 5 minutes in an hour
Answer and explanation:	12 × 2°C = 24°C 4°C – 24°C = **-20°C**

Question:	5) Ann puts £30 into her bank account. She now has £18. How much money was she previously in debt by?
Think about 'What I Need' (WIN) first	

Question:	6) The temperature in Moscow is -10°C and in London it is 3°C. What is the difference between the temperatures?
WIN:	

Question:	7) i) Put the numbers in order to find the median: -11, 3, 1, -1, 0, -6, -2 ii) What is the range of these numbers?
WIN:	

Question:	8) Temperature decreases at an average of 3°C every 4 minutes. If the temperature is 40°C, what will the temperature be after an hour?
WIN:	

Co-ordinates, shape and negative numbers

Question:	Mark and label the missing co-ordinates on this rectangle:
	(graph showing points at approximately (-3,2), (2,2), (2,-1))
WIN:	Know that *x*-axis is *across* (horizontal) and *y*-axis is *up* (vertical)
WIN:	Use the other co-ordinates to find the fourth So, (-4, -1)

Question:	9) Mark and label the missing co-ordinates for this square:
Think about 'What **I** Need' (**WIN**) first	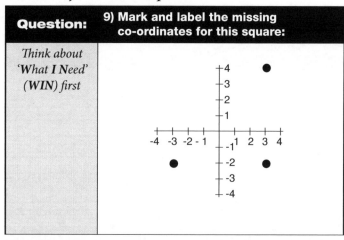

Question:	Label C on this isosceles trapezium:
	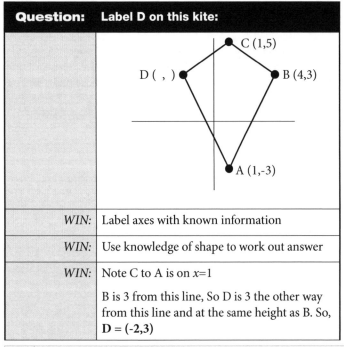 D (-2,1) C A (-4,-2) B (5,-2)
WIN:	Know that an isosceles trapezium is a quadrilateral with a bisecting line of symmetry
WIN:	Label the axes with known information
WIN:	It is important to note the range of the *x* co-ordinate of A and D which is -4 to -2 = 2 So, the gap of the *x* co-ordinate of B and C is 2. Hence: B is 5 – 2 = 3 C *x* co-ordinate is 3 and it is 1 *up* as shown by the *y* co-ordinate of D. **C = (3,1)**

Question:	10) Label C on this isosceles triangle:
WIN:	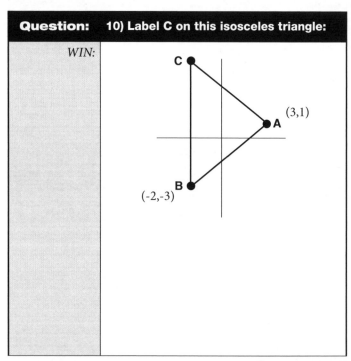

Question:	Label D on this kite:
	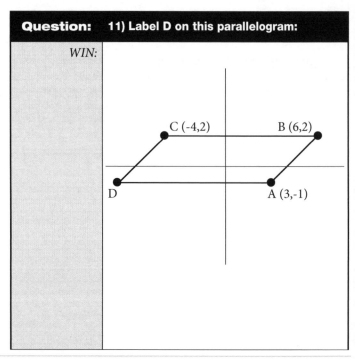 C (1,5) D (,) B (4,3) A (1,-3)
WIN:	Label axes with known information
WIN:	Use knowledge of shape to work out answer
WIN:	Note C to A is on *x*=1 B is 3 from this line, So D is 3 the other way from this line and at the same height as B. So, **D = (-2,3)**

Question:	11) Label D on this parallelogram:
WIN:	C (-4,2) B (6,2) D A (3,-1)

Negative integers, co-ordinates, algebra and translation

Now it is your turn to practise...

Question:	i) Write the plotted co-ordinates to find the rule that connects them ii) Write the formula for the line
	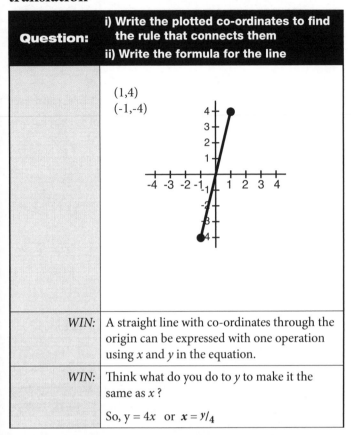 (1,4) (-1,-4)
WIN:	A straight line with co-ordinates through the origin can be expressed with one operation using x and y in the equation.
WIN:	Think what do you do to y to make it the same as x ? So, $y = 4x$ or $x = y/4$

Question:	Write the formula for the x and y co-ordinates:
	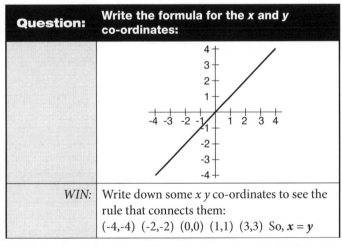
WIN:	Write down some $x\,y$ co-ordinates to see the rule that connects them: (-4,-4) (-2,-2) (0,0) (1,1) (3,3) So, $x = y$

Question:	Translate the rectangle (3,1):
	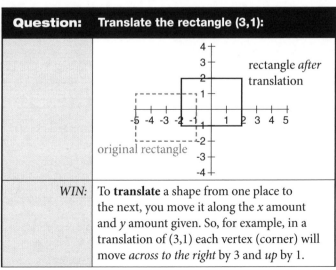 rectangle *after* translation original rectangle
WIN:	To **translate** a shape from one place to the next, you move it along the x amount and y amount given. So, for example, in a translation of (3,1) each vertex (corner) will move *across to the right* by 3 and *up* by 1.

Question:	12) i) Write the plotted co-ordinates to find the rule that connects them ii) Write the formula for the line
Think about 'What I Need' (WIN) first	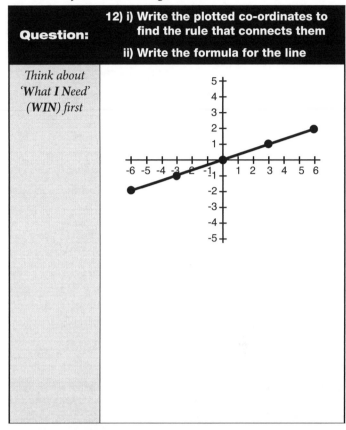

Question:	13) Write the formula for the x, y co-ordinates:
WIN:	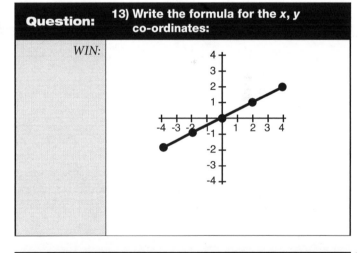

Question:	14) Translate the square by (2,1):
WIN:	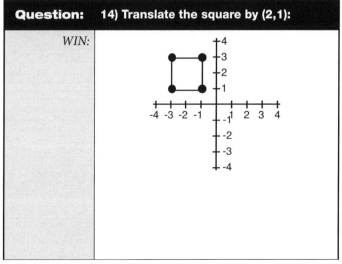

Shapes, angles and area with sorting data

Triangles, quadrilaterals and sorting information

Question:	1) Place 5 out of the 6 shapes in the carroll diagram:

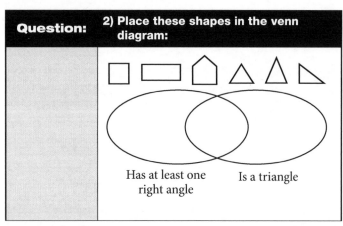

	Has 4 right angles	Does not have right angles
Has 2 pairs of same length sides		
Has equal length sides		

rectangle
rhombus
kite

parallelogram   square   trapezium

WIN:	**Parallel** = ══════
	Perpendicular = ⌐
	A **trapezium** has one pair of parallel sides.
	A **rhombus** is a parallelogram with four equal length sides.

Question:	2) Place these shapes in the venn diagram:

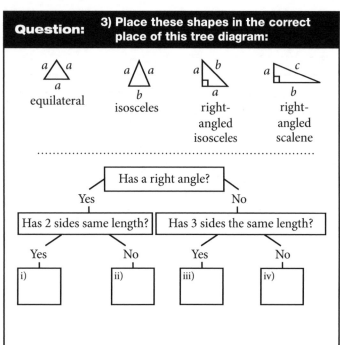

Has at least one right angle   Is a triangle

Question:	3) Place these shapes in the correct place of this tree diagram:

$a\triangle a$
a
equilateral

$a\triangle a$
b
isosceles

$a\triangle b$
a
right-angled isosceles

$a\triangle c$
b
right-angled scalene

Has a right angle?
Yes   No
Has 2 sides same length?   Has 3 sides the same length?
Yes   No   Yes   No
i)   ii)   iii)   iv)

Angles

Question:	4) i/ii/iii) Find the missing angles:

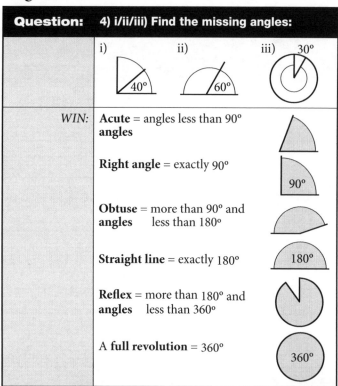

i)   40°   ii)   60°   iii)   30°

WIN:	**Acute** = angles less than 90° **angles**
	Right angle = exactly 90° 90°
	Obtuse = more than 90° and **angles** less than 180°
	Straight line = exactly 180° 180°
	Reflex = more than 180° and **angles** less than 360°
	A **full revolution** = 360° 360°

Question:	5) i/ii/iii) Find the missing angles:

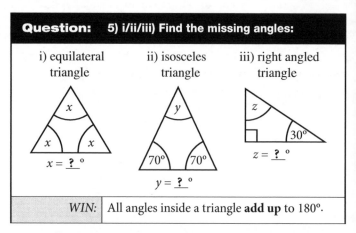

i) equilateral triangle   ii) isosceles triangle   iii) right angled triangle

x
x x
$x = \underline{?}°$

y
$70°$ $70°$
$y = \underline{?}°$

z
$30°$
$z = \underline{?}°$

WIN:	All angles inside a triangle **add up** to 180°.

Question:	6) i/ii) Find the missing angles:

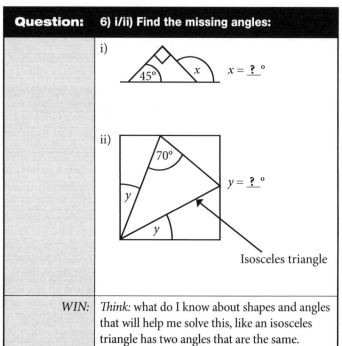

i)   45° x $x = \underline{?}°$

ii)   70° y $y = \underline{?}°$ y

Isosceles triangle

WIN:	*Think:* what do I know about shapes and angles that will help me solve this, like an isosceles triangle has two angles that are the same.

Area and perimeter of squares, rectangles and area of parallelograms and compound shapes

Question:	7) Calculate the area of this parallelogram:
	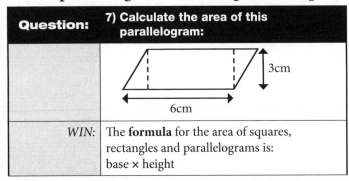
WIN:	The **formula** for the area of squares, rectangles and parallelograms is: base × height

Question:	8) i/ii) Find the area and perimeter of: iii) Find the length *x*:
	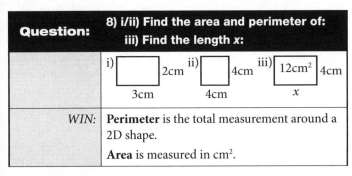
WIN:	**Perimeter** is the total measurement around a 2D shape. **Area** is measured in cm².

Question:	9) Find the area and perimeter of:
	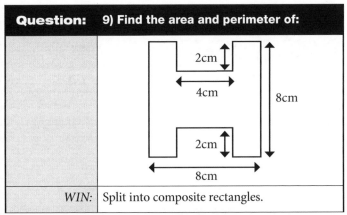
WIN:	Split into composite rectangles.

Question:	10) Paving stones are sold as *standard* and *large*. They can be arranged as shown below. If the area of a standard stone is 128cm², what are the dimensions of the large stone?
	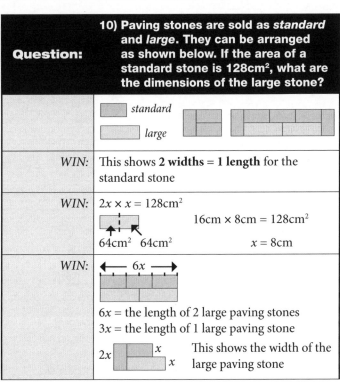
WIN:	This shows **2 widths = 1 length** for the standard stone
WIN:	$2x \times x = 128\text{cm}^2$ ... $16\text{cm} \times 8\text{cm} = 128\text{cm}^2$ ... 64cm^2 64cm^2 ... $x = 8\text{cm}$
WIN:	6x = the length of 2 large paving stones. 3x = the length of 1 large paving stone. This shows the width of the large paving stone

Areas of triangles and compound shapes

Question:	11) i/ii/iii) Find the area of these triangles:
	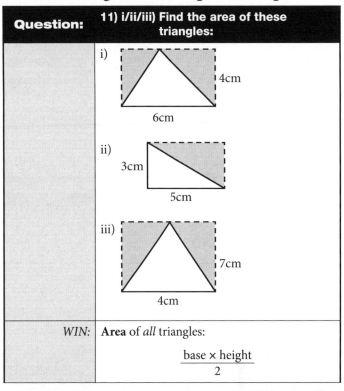
WIN:	**Area** of *all* triangles: $$\frac{\text{base} \times \text{height}}{2}$$

Question:	12) i/ii/iii) Find the height of these triangles:
	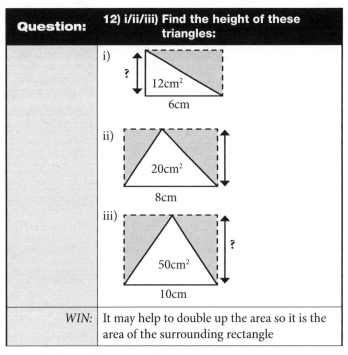
WIN:	It may help to double up the area so it is the area of the surrounding rectangle

Question:	13) Find the area of:
	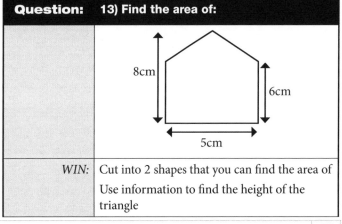
WIN:	Cut into 2 shapes that you can find the area of. Use information to find the height of the triangle

Angles, factor pairs, area, nets, volume and symmetry

Factor pairs, area of rectangles and perimeter

Question:	1) Write the factor pairs for 24.
WIN:	**Factors** are numbers that go into other numbers with no remainder For example, **Factor pairs** of 6, are: 1, 6, 2, 3 **Factors** of 6, are: 1, 2, 3, and 6

Question:	2) Draw all the possible rectangles (that is with different length sides) which have an area of 24cm².
WIN:	**Area** of rectangles = base × height For example, Rectangles with an area of 6cm² are: 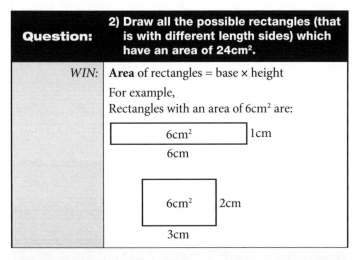

Question:	3) If this whole shape has an area of 200cm², what is the perimeter of one square?
	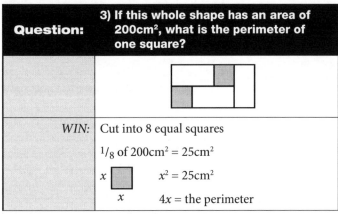
WIN:	Cut into 8 equal squares $1/8$ of 200cm² = 25cm² x ▢ $x^2 = 25$cm² x $4x$ = the perimeter

Question:	4) Design a 'Mondrian' in an 8 x 8cm grid (see example below).
	Blue rectangles have an area of 2cm² Yellow rectangles and squares have an area of 4cm² Red rectangles have an area of 8cm² White rectangles and squares have an area of 16cm² 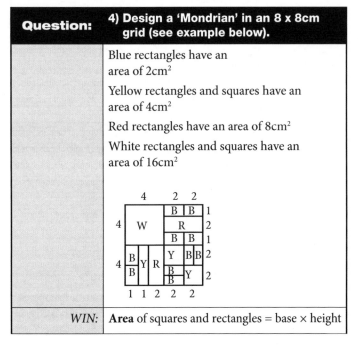
WIN:	**Area** of squares and rectangles = base × height

Angles

Question:	5) Use two lines of card joined in the centre with a split pin: What can you show about angles?
	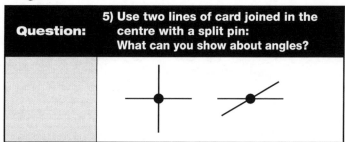

Question:	6) Use four equal length lines of card joined in the corners with four split pins: What can you show about angles?
	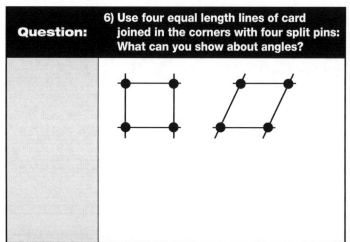

Question:	7) Use the information below to work out the total interior angles of an octagon (8 sided shape):

Shape	Edges	Total of interior angles
Triangle	3	180°
Square	4	360°
Pentagon	5	540°
Hexagon	6	720°
Heptagon	7	900°

Question:	8) Find angle x in this regular pentagon
	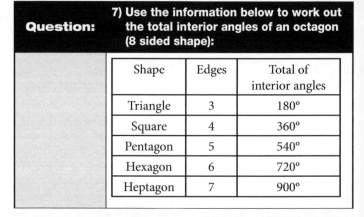
WIN:	Angles around a point = 360° 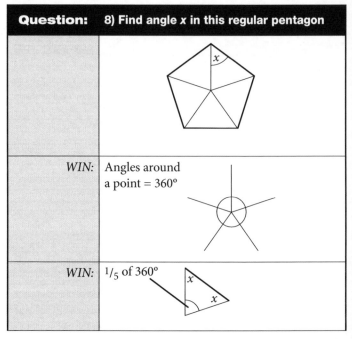
WIN:	$1/5$ of 360°

Nets, 3D shapes, protractor use, volume and surface area

Question:	9) Match the net to the shape:

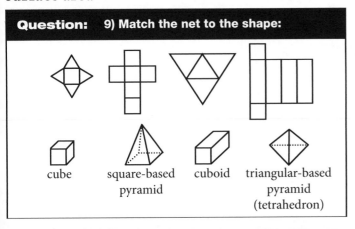

cube   square-based pyramid   cuboid   triangular-based pyramid (tetrahedron)

Question:	10) Use a protractor and ruler to draw this net of a triangular-based pyramid:

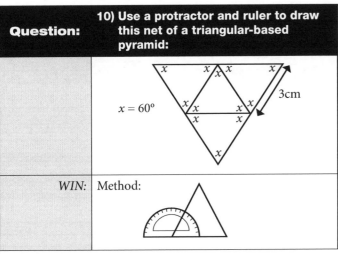

$x = 60°$

3cm

WIN:	Method:

Question:	11) Find the volume and surface area:

i)
ii)

1cm   3cm
2cm

iii)
iv)

2cm
3cm
4cm

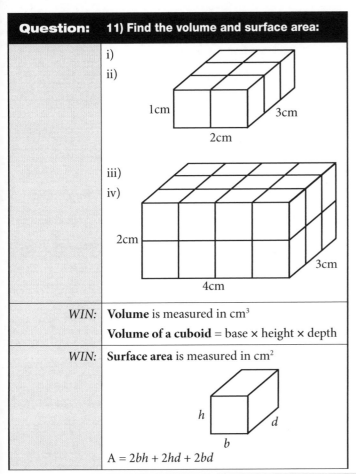

WIN:	**Volume** is measured in cm³ **Volume of a cuboid** = base × height × depth
WIN:	**Surface area** is measured in cm² $A = 2bh + 2hd + 2bd$

h d b

Symmetry: reflective and rotational

Question:	12) Use a grid to draw your own design with reflective symmetry (with one mirror line) – see example.
Example:	

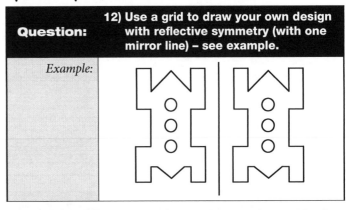

Question:	13) Use a quadrant to draw your design with reflective symmetry (with two mirror lines) – see example:
Example:	

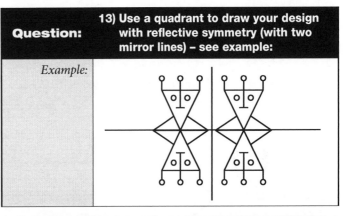

Question:	14) Use a quadrant to support your design with rotational symmetry with an order of 4
Example:	

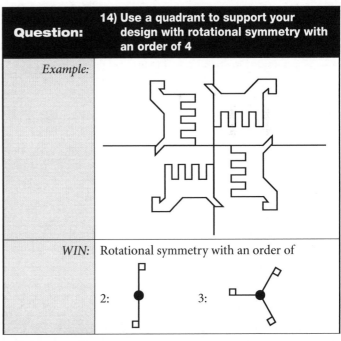

WIN:	Rotational symmetry with an order of 2: 3:

Question:	15) Complete this design so it has rotational symmetry with an order of 2 about point A

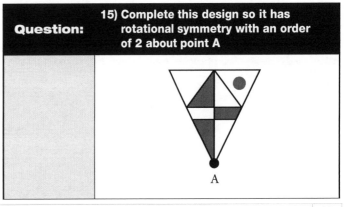

A

Averages, collecting and interpreting data, charts and graphs

Averages: mode, mean, median and range

Now it is your turn to practise...

Question:	Find the mode of: 1, 1, 2, 4
WIN:	The **mode** is the value that occurs *most* often
Answer and explanation:	1, 1, 2, 4 = **1**

Question:	1) Find the mode of these prices: 99p, 99p, £2.00, £2.00, £2.00
Think about 'What I Need' (WIN) first	

Question:	Find the mean of: £2.00, £4.00, £6.00
WIN:	To find the **mean,** add up all the values and divide by the number of values
Answer and explanation:	£2.00, £4.00, £6.00 = £12.00 $\dfrac{£12.00}{3\ (values)}$ = **£4.00**

Question:	2) Find the mean of: £1.00, £3.00, £5.00
WIN:	

Question:	Find the median of: 2, 1, 3
WIN:	The **median** is the *middle* value for a set of data that is in numerical order
Answer and explanation:	1, 2, 3 = **2**

Question:	3) Find the median of: 5, 1, 3
WIN:	

Question:	Find the median of: 1, 3, 5, 9
WIN:	If there is an even set of numbers, find the median by adding the *middle two numbers* together and dividing by two
Answer and explanation:	1, 3, 5, 9 is $\dfrac{3+5}{2}$ = **4**

Question:	4) Find the median of: 1, 2, 4, 6
WIN:	

Question:	Find the range of the numbers: 3, 1, 20
WIN:	The **range** is the difference between the highest and lowest value
Answer and explanation:	3, 1, 20 is 20–1 = **19**

Question:	5) Find the range of the numbers: 2, 1, 10
WIN:	

Question:	Write 3 numbers that have a mean of 5, a mode of 4, a median of 4, and a range of 3.
WIN:	Use what you know about mode, mean, median and range to solve this
Answer and explanation:	The total of 3 numbers with of mean of 5 is 15 Two numbers must be 4 as that is the mode **4 4 7**

Question:	6) Write 7 numbers that have a mean of 9, a mode of 5, a median of 10, and a range of 18.
WIN:	☐ ☐ ☐ ☐ ☐ ☐ ☐

Collecting and interpreting data

Question:	Complete the conversion table:

Oliver Island (£)	£1		£7	
British (£)	£3	£12		£102

WIN:	Find the rule that connects the Oliver Island pound and the British pound

Answer and explanation:	

Oliver Island £ ⇄ British £ (× 3 / ÷ 3)

Oliver Island (£)	£1	£4	£7	£34
British (£)	£3	£12	£21	£102

Question:	Look at the bus timetable. Bus 1 gets caught in traffic and is 35 minutes late reaching C. At what time does it arrive at C?

	Bus 1	Bus 2
A	09:00	12:30
B	10:15	13:40
C	11:40	15:00
D	13:05	16:20
E	15:25	18:10

WIN:	The 24 hour clock. Add 12 for pm times.

Answer and explanation:	11:40 add 35 minutes

$11:40 \xrightarrow{20\ mins} 12:00 \xrightarrow{15\ mins} \mathbf{12:15}$

Question:	Complete the tally chart for the data in the pie chart:

Colour of cars that passed the school in one hour

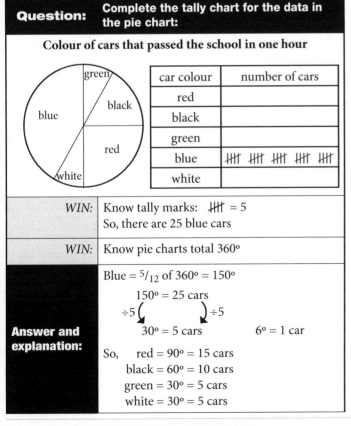

car colour	number of cars
red	
black	
green	
blue	|||| |||| |||| |||| ||||
white	

WIN:	Know tally marks: |||| = 5 So, there are 25 blue cars

WIN:	Know pie charts total 360°

Answer and explanation:	Blue = $^5/_{12}$ of 360° = 150°

150° = 25 cars

÷5 (30° = 5 cars) ÷5   6° = 1 car

So, red = 90° = 15 cars
black = 60° = 10 cars
green = 30° = 5 cars
white = 30° = 5 cars

Now it is your turn to practise...

Question:	7) Complete the conversion table of Martian pounds to British pounds. 1 Martian pound = £1.25

Martian (£)	£1		£25	
British (£)		£3.75		£62.50

Question:	8) i) Which bus takes least time to get from A to E? ii) How long is the average journey time from point D to E?

	Bus 1	Bus 2
A	09:00	12:30
B	10:15	13:40
C	11:40	15:00
D	13:05	16:20
E	15:25	18:10

9) There are two spinners

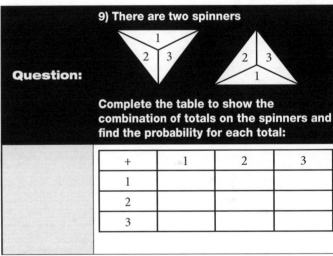

Question:	Complete the table to show the combination of totals on the spinners and find the probability for each total:

+	1	2	3
1			
2			
3			

Question:	10) Complete the tally chart for the data in the pie chart:

car colour	number of cars
red	|||| ||||
black	
green	
blue	
white	||||

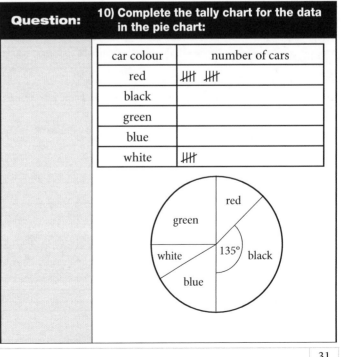

Pie charts, bar charts and line graphs

Question:	Use the pie chart to find out how many children, out of 40, like Maths the most:
	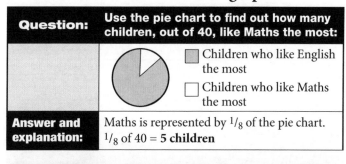 Children who like English the most / Children who like Maths the most
Answer and explanation:	Maths is represented by $1/_8$ of the pie chart. $1/_8$ of 40 = **5 children**

Question:	Children like chocolate in the ratio milk : dark : white 6 : 5 : 1 Draw a pie chart to show this ratio
WIN:	6 + 5 + 1 = 12 parts
WIN:	360° around a point
Answer and explanation:	360° around a point divided by 12 parts = 30° for each part So, 6 × 30° = **180°** 5 × 30° = **150°** 1 × 30° = **30°**

Question:	Look at the bar chart for the shoe sizes worn by the girls and boys in 6A i) How many children are in the class? ii) What is the mode shoe size for girls? iii) What is the mode shoe size for boys?
	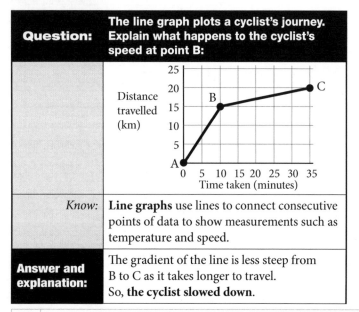
WIN:	The **mode** is the value that occurs *most* often
Answer and explanation:	Total number of children = **30** Mode shoe size for girls = **2** Mode shoe size for boys = **4**

Question:	The line graph plots a cyclist's journey. Explain what happens to the cyclist's speed at point B:
	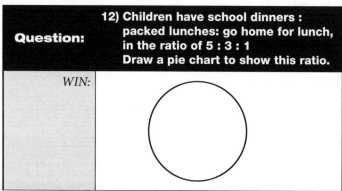
Know:	**Line graphs** use lines to connect consecutive points of data to show measurements such as temperature and speed.
Answer and explanation:	The gradient of the line is less steep from B to C as it takes longer to travel. So, **the cyclist slowed down.**

Now it is your turn to practise...

Question:	11) Compare the pie charts and explain why school A has a greater number of children who have school dinners than school B:
	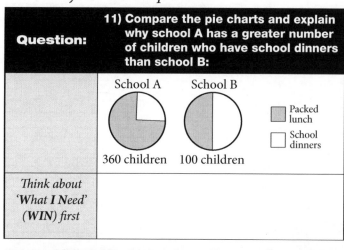 School A / School B — 360 children / 100 children — Packed lunch / School dinners
Think about 'What I Need' (WIN) first	

Question:	12) Children have school dinners : packed lunches: go home for lunch, in the ratio of 5 : 3 : 1 Draw a pie chart to show this ratio.
WIN:	⭕

Question:	13) Look at the bar chart and explain the trend of shoe sizes worn by the girls and boys in 6A
	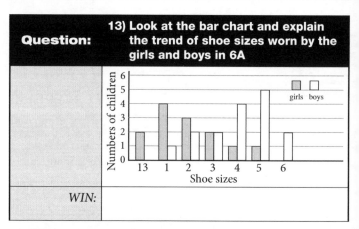
WIN:	

Question:	14) Explain what is happening (lines A–B, B–C, C–D) when someone travels on the cycle ride shown by the line graph below:
	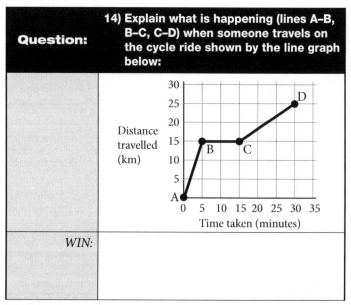
WIN:	

Representing data badly

Question:	The school five-a-side football team needs to buy new shirts. The players wear the following (chest-size) shirts:

player 1 69cm	player 2 69cm	player 3 71cm	player 4 81cm	player 5 74cm

Explain which average (mode, mean, median or range) is most useful to decide on the strategy for choosing sizes to buy.

WIN:	Consider what the averages show in actual 'real' terms. The modal size is 69cm but the other children are larger and will not fit in small shirts. The mean and median value again will not accommodate the larger children.
Answer and explanation:	The range shows the huge difference in the sizes and shows a range of sizes must therefore be bought.

Question:	Favourite crisp flavours of a class are represented by the pie and bar charts. Explain which chart is better at representing this data:

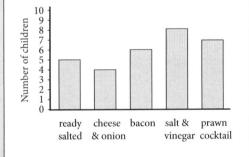

Answer and explanation:	The bar chart is better at representing favourite crisp flavours because it is possible to see the actual amount of children favouring a flavour and accurately see the most favourite with data that has such a small range.

Now it is your turn to practise...

15) The salary of five people from Oliver Island is used to decide whether there is a good standard of living. With costs of living, it is decided 15,000 oliver pounds represents a reasonable salary.

King	Ø£200,000
Woodcutter	Ø£6,000
Teacher	Ø£15,000
Doctor	Ø£23,000
Chef	Ø£6,000

Question:	Use the information and the following statements to decide which average (mode, mean, median) has been used by each speaker to comment on the standard of living and explain how you know.

a) "The average salary is more than a reasonable salary. So, the people live well."

b) "Most people are extremely poor and struggle to survive."

c) "People earn a reasonable salary that can accommodate the cost of living. So, they can afford what they need."

Think about 'What I Need' (WIN) first	

Question:	**16)** Decide which chart or graph is the best way to represent the mean monthly temperatures for Oliver Island and draw it.

Mean monthly temperatures for Oliver Island												
	J	F	M	A	M	J	J	A	S	O	N	D
°C	20	19	17	15	12	10	9	10	11	14	17	19

WIN:	

ANSWERS

The four operations, one-step to multi-step problems

1) **12p**   2) **48p**   3) **52p**

4) **£2.80**   5) **£2.16**   6) **£9.72**

7)
$$\begin{array}{r} 25 \\ \times\ 16 \\ \hline 150 \\ 250 \leftarrow \\ \hline 400 \end{array}$$
The answer is wrong because a zero needs to be put in the units column as we are multiplying 25 by 10, not 1.

8) **3 adults**   9) **£12.90**   10) **£1.29**

11) $23 \times 10 = 230$
$23 \times 20 = 460$ (23×30)
$23 \times 30 = 690$
$$\begin{array}{r} 736 \\ -\ 690 \\ \hline 46 \end{array} = (23 \times 2)$$
$726 \div 23 = 32$

12) **Because it is impossible to have 1.5 egg boxes so 2 boxes would be needed but there would be 3 empty spaces in the second box.**

13) **£4.23**   14) **£1.61**   15) **£5.50**

16) **£2.00**

Multiplying/dividing by 10,100,1000, conversion, money and 10%

1) **Move all digits right three places**

2i) **0.19m, 21cm, 220mm**

2ii) **0.7km, 710m, 7000m**

3) **999,999mm or 0.999999km**

4) **10 minutes**

5i/ii)
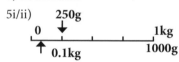

6) **Answers will vary**

7)
in	1	2	10	40
cm	2.54	5.08	25.4	101.6

kg	1	2	5	10
lbs	2.2	4.4	11	22

litre	1	2	10	40
pints	1.8	3.6	18	72

8)
Stone	1	2	3	4	5
Kg	6.35	12.7	19.05	25.4	31.75

Personal weight will vary.

9)
litre	cl	ml
2	200	2000
3.5	350	3500
4.8	480	4800

10) **8**   11) **2.7 litres**

12i) $\frac{1}{2}$ 12ii) $\frac{6}{25}$ 12iii) $\frac{7}{20}$

12iv) $\frac{3}{4}$ 13i) **17p**   13ii) **£9.30**

14i) **7p**   14ii) **70p**   14iii) **21p**

14iv) **£2.10**   15) **£40.50**   16) **£50**

Fractions, percentages and decimals

1i) **6**   1ii) **12**   1iii) **15**

1iv) **30**   2i) **32**   2ii) **56**

2iii) **72**   2iv) **60**   3i) **2**

3ii) **6**   3iii) **114**   3iv) **188**

4) **160**   5i) $\frac{n}{2}$ or $\frac{n}{100} \times 50$

5ii) $\frac{n}{4}$ or $\frac{n}{100} \times 25$

5iii) $\frac{3n}{4}$ or $\frac{n}{100} \times 75$ 6i) $\frac{n}{100}$

6ii) $\frac{23n}{100}$ or $\frac{n}{100} \times 23$

6iii) $\frac{67n}{100}$ or $\frac{n}{100} \times 67$

There are several alternative formulae to show how to find percentages using n (5,6&7)

7i) **For example:** $\frac{n}{20}$ or $\frac{n}{100} \times 5$

7ii) $\frac{n}{20} \times 3$ or $\frac{n}{100} \times 15$

8i) **144**   8ii) **648**

9i) $\frac{1}{10}$ **10% 0.1**   9ii) $\frac{1}{2}$ **50% 0.5**

9iii) $\frac{1}{4}$ **25% 0.25**   9iv) $\frac{3}{4}$ **75% 0.75**

9v) $\frac{1}{100}$ **1% 0.01**   9vi) $\frac{2}{5}$ **40% 0.4**

10i) $\frac{1}{8} > 0.12$ 10ii) $\frac{1}{7} > 0.14$

10iii) **0.11 = 11%**   11i) $\frac{7}{10}$

11ii) $\frac{3}{10}$ 11iii) $\frac{1}{10}$ 11iv) $\frac{5}{2}$ or **2.5**

12i) **4**   12ii) $7\frac{1}{3}$ or $7.\dot{3}$

12iii) **7**   12iv) $6\frac{1}{2}$ or **6.5**

13i) **42p**   13ii) **84p**   13iii) **30p**

13iv) **90p**   14) **450**   15) **150**

Fractions, probability, ratio and proportion

1i)   1ii)

2i) **1:3**   2ii) **2:3**

3i) $\frac{1}{5}$ **shaded,** $\frac{4}{5}$ **unshaded**

3ii) $\frac{1}{3}$ **shaded,** $\frac{2}{3}$ **unshaded**

4i)    4ii) **1:5**

5i) $\frac{2}{6} = \frac{1}{3}$ 5ii) **2:3**   6i) **12**

6ii) $\frac{2}{5}$ 7) **1:6** $\frac{6}{7}$ 8) $\frac{1}{2} \times \frac{1}{2} = \frac{1}{4}$ 9i) **£4:£6**

9ii) **£16:£24**   9iii) **£14:£21**   10i) **30**

10ii) **132**   11) **35**   12i) **10:2:5**

12ii) **£10**   13) **300ml**   14) **88km**

15i) **62**   15ii) **248°**   16i) **360g**

16ii) **75p**

Equations, sequences, finding rules and formulae

1i) $x = 6$ 1ii) $y = 20$ 1iii) $5z = 35$

2i) $x = 3$ 2ii) $y = 10$ 2iii) $5z = 35$

3) $11n = 77cm$, $n = 7cm$

4) $n + 2n + 4 = 3n + 4$, $3n + 4 = 34$, $n = 10$

5i) **10, 12**   5ii) **40,50**   6i) **-11, -15**

6ii) $\frac{1}{8}, \frac{1}{16}$ 6iii) **Because the numbers are decreasing by 3 and all numbers are in the '3' times-tables, including 3**

7) **94**   8) **15, 18, 20, 23, 25**

9) **× 4** $4n$ 10) **× 5** $5n$

11) **× 2 + 1** $2n + 1$ **10 → 21**

12) $1 \to 4$, $2 \to 7$, $3 \to 10$

13) $1 \to 2$, $2 \to 9$, $3 \to 28$, $10 \to 1001$

14) $20 \to 1$, $30 \to 1.5$, $40 \to 2$ 15) $\frac{n}{20}$

Negative numbers, co-ordinates and translation

1) -3   2) -3   3) -5
  -2   4   -3
  -1   8   -5
   0   13   -3
   1

4i) **100**   4ii) **-100**   4iii) **-100**

4iv) **100**   5) **£12**   6) **13°C**

7i) **-11, -6, -2, -1, 0, 1, 3 Median is -1**

7ii) **Range is 14**   8) **-5°C**

9)
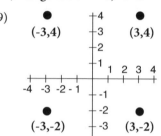
(-3,4)   (3,4)
(-3,-2)   (3,-2)

10) $C = (-2,5)$ 11) $D = (-7,-1)$

12i) **(-6,-2), (-3,-1), (0,0), (3,1), (6,2)**

12ii) $3y = x$ **or** $y = \frac{x}{3}$

13) $x = 2y$ **or** $y = \frac{x}{2}$

14)
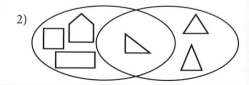

Shapes, angles and area with sorting data

1)
rectangle	parallelogram kite
square	rhombus

2)
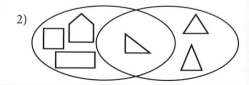

ANSWERS

3i) **right-angled isosceles**
ii) **right-angled scalene**
iii) **equilateral**
iv) **isosceles**

4i) **50°** 4ii) **120°**
4iii) **330°** 5i) **x = 60°**
5ii) **y = 40°** 5iii) **z = 60°**
6i) **x = 135°** 6ii) **y = 25°**

7) **18cm²**

8i) **Area = 6cm², Perimeter = 10cm**
ii) **Area = 16cm², Perimeter = 16cm**
iii) **x = 3cm**

9i) **Area = 48cm², Perimeter = 40cm**

10) **24cm × 8cm**

11i) **12cm²** 11ii) **7.5cm²**
11iii) **14cm²** 12i) **4cm**
12ii) **5cm** 12iii) **10cm**

13) **35cm²**

Angles, factor pairs, area, nets, volume and symmetry

1) **1,24; 2,12; 3,8; 4,6**

2)
2cm / 12cm
3cm / 8cm
1cm / 24cm
4cm / 6cm
(These answers are shown not to scale)

3) **20cm**

4)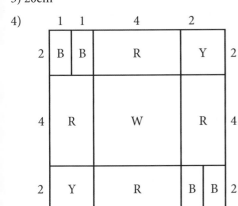
One possible answer shown above, (several alternatives are possible)

5) **Opposite angles are equal**

6) **Opposite angles are equal**

7) **1080°** 8) **x = 54°**

9) 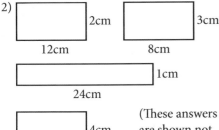 **Square-based pyramid**

Cube

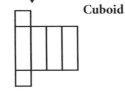 Triangular-based pyramid (tetrahedron)

 **Cuboid**

10) **Check accuracy by checking if it makes a tetrahedron.**

11i) **6cm³** ii) **22cm²**
ii) **24cm³** iv) **52cm²**

12)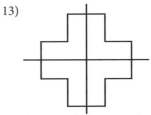
One possible answer shown above, (several alternatives are possible)

13)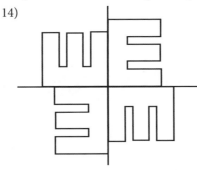
One possible answer shown above, (several alternatives are possible)

14)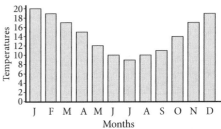
One possible answer shown above, (several alternatives are possible)

15)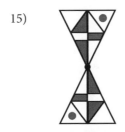

Data handling

1) **£2.00** 2) **£3.00** 3) **3**
4) **3** 5) **9**
6) **1, 5, 5, 10, 11, 12, 19**

7)
Martian	£1	£3	£25	£50
British	£1.25	£3.75	£31.25	£62.50

8i) **Bus 2** 8ii) **2 hours and 5 minutes**

9)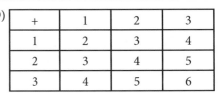
+	1	2	3
1	2	3	4
2	3	4	5
3	4	5	6

Total 2 = ¹/₉ Total 3 = ²/₉
Total 4 = ³/₉ = ¹/₃ Total 5 = ²/₉
Total 6 = ¹/₉

10)
black: 135° = 30 cars ⤑⤑⤑⤑⤑⤑
green: 90° = 20 cars ⤑⤑⤑⤑
blue: 67.5° = 15 cars ⤑⤑⤑

11) ¹/₄ of 360 = 90, ¹/₂ of 100 = 50

12)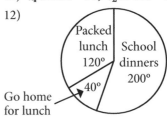

13) **Boys tend to wear larger shoes.**

14) **A–B: speed is 180km/hr (fast)**
B–C: stationary for 10 minutes
C–D: speed is 40km/hr (slow)

15) *Mean:* **All salaries add up to Ø£250,000, giving a mean salary of Ø£50,000 which is well above the salary regarded as reasonable.**
Mode: **The mode salary is Ø£6,000, even though more people have reasonable salary or above.**
Median: **When the salaries are arranged in order, Ø£15,000 is the average, which is the salary regarded as reasonable.**

16) **A bar chart is a good choice.**
The bar chart needs a title and two labelled axes. Scale must be decided on – that is, what gap should represent how much temperature.
The gaps must go up in constant increments.
A line graph is another good choice, with temperature joined by lines that again clearly indicate the rise and fall in temperatures.
A pie chart would actually not show anything useful.

Mean monthly temperature for Oliver Island

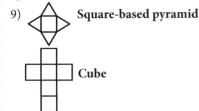

Number

Place value

Question:	What is added to 0.016 to make $^1/_{10}$?
Know number bonds to 100	Number bonds, for example: $90 + 10 = 100$ $84 + 16 = 100$
Place value	Know the value of columns units tenths hundredths thousandths 0.016
Converting hundredths to thousandths	Know that $0.016 = ^1/_{100} + ^6/_{1000}$ $^1/_{100} = ^{10}/_{1000}$ So, $0.016 = ^{10}/_{1000} + ^6/_{1000} = ^{16}/_{1000}$
Answer and explanation:	$^{100}/_{1000} = ^1/_{10} = 0.1$ $^{16}/_{1000} + ^{84}/_{1000} = ^{100}/_{1000}$ or $\begin{array}{r} 0.016 \\ + 0.084 \\ \hline 0.100 \end{array}$ $0.1 - 0.016 = \mathbf{0.084}$

Equivalent fractions

Question:	If $^1/_3$ and $^1/_4$ of an amount total £12.25, what is the amount?
What is $^1/_3$ and $^1/_4$?	$^1/_3$ $^1/_4$ one out of three equal parts — one out of four equal parts
What is $^1/_3$ or $^1/_4$ of an amount?	$^1/_3$ = one part out of three, so divide by 3 eg. $^1/_3$ of 12 = 4 $^1/_4$ = one part out of four, so divide by 4 eg. $^1/_4$ of 12 = 3
How to find equivalent fractions in order to add them	$3 \times 4 = 12$ So $^1/_3$ and $^1/_4$ can be expressed as twelfths To find an equivalent fraction multiply the denominator and numerator by the same number $^1/_3 \xrightarrow{\times 4} {}^4/_{12}$ $^1/_4 \xrightarrow{\times 3} {}^3/_{12}$ $^4/_{12} + ^3/_{12} = ^7/_{12}$
Answer and explanation:	$^1/_3 + ^1/_4 = ^7/_{12} = £12.25$ $^1/_{12} = £12.25 \div 7 = £1.75$ $^{12}/_{12} = £1.75 \times 12 = \mathbf{£21.00}$

Percentages

Question:	If 60% of an amount is £42, what is the amount?
Percent	Percent means out of 100
Percentages and fractions	60% is $^{60}/_{100} = ^6/_{10}$
Finding a fraction of a fraction	To find $^1/_{10}$ from $^6/_{10}$ divide by 6 $^6/_{10}$ 60% £42
Answer and explanation:	$£42 \div 6 = £7$ $^1/_{10} \times 10 = ^{10}/_{10}$ (the whole amount) $£7 \times 10 = \mathbf{£70}$

Money problem using different operations

Question:	A pizza and two colas cost £3.50. Two pizzas and two colas cost £6.20. How much are three pizzas and three colas?
Represent items as letters if it supports finding the answer	$p + 2c = £3.50$ $2p + 2c = £6.20$ $p = £6.20 - £3.50$
Subtraction	Align the point between the pounds and ten pence columns to subtract $\begin{array}{r} £6.20 \\ - £3.50 \\ \hline £2.70 \end{array}$ = cost of one pizza £2.70 + two colas = £3.50 Two colas = £3.50 − £2.70 = 80p 80p ÷ 2 = 40p (one cola)
Long multiplication	$\begin{array}{r} £2.70 \\ \times\ \ 3 \\ \hline £8.10 \end{array}$ $\begin{array}{r} 40 \\ \times\ 3 \\ \hline £1.20 \end{array}$
Answer and explanation:	$\begin{array}{r} £8.10\ = 3p \\ + £1.20\ = 3c \\ \hline £9.30 \end{array}$

Algebra

Formulae from co-ordinates

Question:	Write a formula that shows the rule connecting the *x* and *y* co-ordinates
	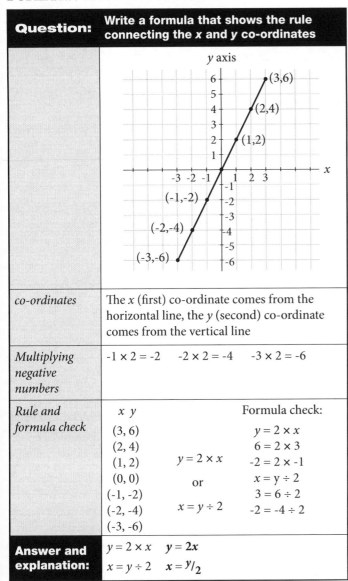
co-ordinates	The *x* (first) co-ordinate comes from the horizontal line, the *y* (second) co-ordinate comes from the vertical line
Multiplying negative numbers	$-1 \times 2 = -2$ $-2 \times 2 = -4$ $-3 \times 2 = -6$
Rule and formula check	$x\ y$ (3, 6) (2, 4) (1, 2) $y = 2 \times x$ (0, 0) or (-1, -2) (-2, -4) $x = y \div 2$ (-3, -6) Formula check: $y = 2 \times x$ $6 = 2 \times 3$ $-2 = 2 \times -1$ $x = y \div 2$ $3 = 6 \div 2$ $-2 = -4 \div 2$
Answer and explanation:	$y = 2 \times x$ $y = 2x$ $x = y \div 2$ $x = y/_2$

Using *n* to find amounts

Question:	In a bag, there are three times as many blue marbles as there are red marbles. There are twice as many green marbles as red marbles. There are two and a half times red marbles as there are yellow marbles. If there are 40 green marbles, how many marbles are there altogether?
Write an equation for the amount of marbles using *n*	Start with the lowest value of marbles (yellow) and call this *n*, then work out how many *n* there are in relation to the yellow marbles yellow red green blue *n* 2.5*n* 5*n* 7.5*n*
Multiply *n* to get rid of any fractions of *n*	yellow red green blue 2*n* 5*n* 10*n* 15*n* $10n = 40$ So, $n = 4$
Find the total *n*	$2n + 5n + 10n + 15n = 32n$
Answer and explanation:	So, $32n = 32 \times 4 = \textbf{128 marbles}$

*n*th term

Question:	Find the *n*th term for 1 ⟶ 9 2 ⟶ 19 3 ⟶ 29 4 ⟶ 39
Rules for sequences	3, 6, 9, 12 × 3 4, 8, 12, 16 × 4
Rules that connect *n* to the resultant number	<table><tr><td>*n*</td><td>1</td><td>2</td><td>3</td><td>4</td></tr><tr><td>resultant number</td><td>2</td><td>4</td><td>6</td><td>8</td></tr></table> Rule = × 2 The rule is the common operation(s) on each *n* to achieve each resultant number
*n*th term and formulae with two operations	*n*th term is the formula that connects *n* to the resultant number <table><tr><td>*n*</td><td>1</td><td>2</td><td>3</td><td>4</td></tr><tr><td>resultant number</td><td>2</td><td>4</td><td>6</td><td>8</td></tr></table> $n \times 2 = 2n$ <table><tr><td>*n*</td><td>1</td><td>2</td><td>3</td><td>4</td></tr><tr><td>resultant number</td><td>3</td><td>5</td><td>7</td><td>9</td></tr></table> $2n + 1$
Answer and explanation:	1 ⟶ 9 10 With a difference of 10, 2 ⟶ 19 10 10*n* is involved, but with 3 ⟶ 29 10 another operation 4 ⟶ 39 10 **10*n*–1**

Using algebra with shape, space and measures

Question:	Find the value of *n*
	triangle with sides $2n$, $3n$, area 27cm^2
Formulae for the area of a rectangle and area of a triangle	rectangle (base, height); triangle (base, height) Area of a rectangle = base × height Area of a triangle = $\dfrac{\text{base} \times \text{height}}{2}$
Turn the area of a triangle into the area of a rectangle for a straightforward sum	$2n$, $3n$, 27cm^2, 27cm^2 $27\text{cm}^2 \times 2 = 54\text{cm}^2$
Factor pairs	Use factors pairs of 54 to find which pair has a number $1^1/_2$ times as much its pair. Factor pairs of 54: 1, 54, 2, 27, 3, 18, 6, 9
Answer and explanation:	$6 \times 1^1/_2 = 9$ $6 \times 9 = 54$ $2n = 6\text{cm}$ $3n = 9\text{cm}$ $6/_2 = 3$ $9/_3 = 3$ **$n = 3\text{cm}$**

Shape, space and measures

Co-ordinates and parallelograms

Question:	Find the fourth co-ordinate (*A*) of the parallelogram
	B (2,3) D (9,3) A C (6,-2)
Parallelograms	Parallelograms have two sets of parallel sides. This means that A to B = C to D A ⟷ B C ⟷ D
Negative numbers	Know the order order of numbers (0,0) 3 2 1 -3 -2 -1 1 2 3 -1 -2 -3
Co-ordinates	Mark what you know on the axes B D 3 -1 6 2 9 A C -2
Answer and explanation:	On *x*-axis, C to D = 9 – 6 = 3 So, A = 2(*x* co-ordinate) –3 = -1 C *y* co-ordinate = -2 So, **A = (-1,-2)**

Scale and conversion

Question:	On a map House A is 4cm from House B. The scale of the map is 1:25,000. What is the real distance of A to B in kilometres?
	A B
Scale	Scale represents real-life measurements with smaller measurements. So, a scale of 1:25,000 1 unit = 25,000 units (on a map) (in real terms) 1cm = 25,000cm 4cm = 100,000cm
Conversion of cm to km	Know how to convert 100,000cm to kilometres (km) 100cm = 1m 1000m = 1km So, 100,000cm = 1km
Multiplication and division in conversion	÷ 100,000 100,000cm 1km × 100,000
Answer and explanation:	A ⟶ B = 4cm 1cm = 25,000cm 4cm = 100,000cm 100,000cm = **1km**

Angles

Question:	Find the angle *x*
	x 140°
Perpendicular	Know that lines perpendicular to each other have a 90° angle between them
Angles on a straight line	40° 140° Angles on a straight line total 180°
Angles of a triangle	50° 40° Angles of a triangle total 180°
Answer and explanation:	50° Angles around a point total 360° 360° – 50° = 310° **x = 310°**

Time

Question:	Four people took from 10:55 to 12:15 to put 1200 leaflets into envelopes. How long would it take five people to put 1200 leaflets into envelopes?
Time	Work out the time gap 5 mins 1 hour 15 mins 10:55 ⟶ 11:00 ⟶ 12:00 ⟶ 12:15 1 hour and 20 minutes
Convert hours to minutes	1 hour and 20 minutes = 60 and 20 minutes = 80 minutes
Count person hours	4 people working 80 minutes each 4 × 80 = 320 minutes of work
Answer and explanation:	320 minutes of work divided by 5 people = **64 minutes**

Data handling

Pie charts and Bar charts

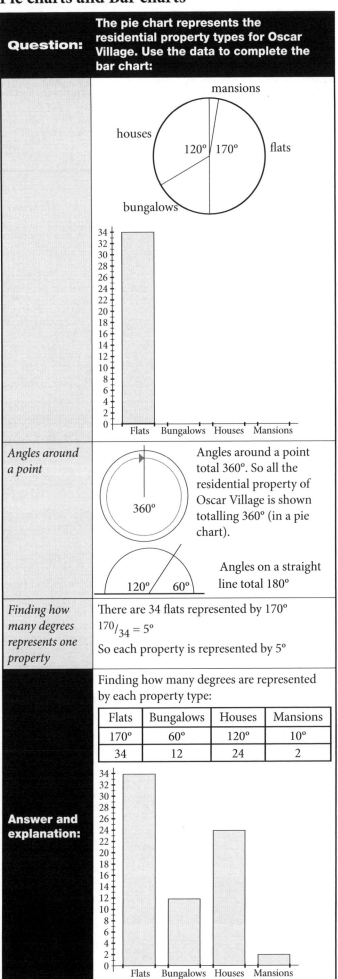

| Question: | The pie chart represents the residential property types for Oscar Village. Use the data to complete the bar chart: |

mansions

houses   120° 170° flats

bungalows

(bar chart with y-axis 0 to 34, x-axis: Flats, Bungalows, Houses, Mansions — Flats bar at 34)

| Angles around a point | Angles around a point total 360°. So all the residential property of Oscar Village is shown totalling 360° (in a pie chart). |

360°

120° / 60° Angles on a straight line total 180°

| Finding how many degrees represents one property | There are 34 flats represented by 170°
$^{170}/_{34} = 5°$
So each property is represented by 5° |

Finding how many degrees are represented by each property type:

Flats	Bungalows	Houses	Mansions
170°	60°	120°	10°
34	12	24	2

| Answer and explanation: | (bar chart: Flats 34, Bungalows 12, Houses 24, Mansions 2) |

Ratio, averages and sorting data

| Question: | There are three houses in a cul-de-sac.

Draw how many people are in each house from the data given below, using:

👤 to show each adult and

👤 to show each child.

• Each house has at least 1 adult in it
• In one house the ratio of adults to children is 5:1
• The mean number of adults per house is 3
• There are five children living in one house
• 3 people from one house go to visit the most east house, which now has five times as many people in it as its next door neighbour |

(diagram of three houses with stick figures; compass showing N, S, E, W)

Adults to children is 5:1
It cannot be 10:2 as the mean number of adults is only 3

People must total 5 as when 3 people visit the east house, there are now 5 times as many people in the east house. Also, it has 2 adults in it as the mean number of adults is 3

The house with 5 children must have an odd number of people in it. So, there must be 2 adults as 3 more people make a total of 10 (five times the remaining two people next door)

| Answer: | (diagram of three houses with stick figures) |

Probability trees

Question:	At the outset there are three red balls and two yellow balls. Complete this probability tree that show two balls being selected without replacement, one after each other, at random.

Representing probability as a fraction	Probability can easily be expressed as a fraction. For example, if there are four white balls and three black balls, there is a $4/7$ chance of picking a white ball and a $3/7$ chance of picking a black ball.
Probability that changes	The probability will change after one ball is taken out, shown by

Probability for more than one action	The probability of two white balls being picked out one after the other is $$4/7 \times 3/6 = 12/42 = 2/7$$ (multiply fractions by multiplying the numerators together and the denominators together)
Answer and explanation:	

Venn diagrams with lowest common multiples

Question:	Complete this venn diagram until the lowest common multiple is included:

Multiple	A multiple of the number is any number that is the product of the number
Lowest common multiple	The lowest common multiple is the smallest multiple that can be exactly divided by every member of a set of numbers. So, the lowest common multiple of 3 and 4 is 12, as 12 is the first multiple of both these numbers.
Venn diagrams and lowest common multiple	Venn diagrams have an overlap for the categories that are common to multiples

Answer and explanation:	

Differentiated word problems: Number

Topic	one-step	two-step	multi-step	creative multi-step
Four operations	Find the missing numbers: $\begin{array}{r} 3\ \square\ 4 \\ +\ \square\ 9\ \square \\ \hline 5\ 4\ 2 \end{array}$	$^{63}/_{14} = ?$	What is half of 0.61 add 0.62?	Find the missing numbers: $6\ \square\ 4 \times 3\ \square = 21216$
Division problems	$45 \div 6 = ?$	Trays hold 6 eggs. How many trays are needed to hold 45 eggs?	There are 6 chocolates in each bag. How many whole bags can be made up of 45 chocolates?	What is $^1/_6$ as a percentage?
Four operations and money	What is the total of two pens costing 36p each?	What is the change from £2 for a pen that costs 43p and a pencil that costs 18p?	If 5 apples cost £1 and 4 bananas cost 60p, how much would 2 apples and 3 bananas cost?	If 3 pens and 2 rulers cost £1.50 and 4 pens and 2 rulers cost £1.90, how much are 5 pens and 3 rulers?
Rounding numbers	Round 3.68 to one decimal place (the nearest tenth)	Round the total of 4.32 and 6.468 to two decimal places (the nearest hundredth)	What is 30682m to the nearest whole km?	What is 6.8l and 5045ml to the nearest whole cl?
Negative numbers, prime numbers, multiples and factors	It is 5°C in London and 23°C colder in Moscow. What is the temperature in Moscow?	What is the product of the first three prime numbers?	What is the lowest common multiple of 2, 3 and 5?	What are the dimensions of a rectangle that has a perimeter of 18cm and an area of 18cm²?
Multiplying and dividing by 10	$3.6 \times 10 =$	Complete: $7 \times 10 =$ $7 \times 1 =$ $7 \times 0.1 =$ $7 \times 0.01 =$	Complete: $7 \div \square = 700$ $7 \div \square = 70$ $7 \div \square = 7$ $7 \div \square = 0.7$	What is interesting about multiplying and dividing by decimal numbers?
Fractions, percentages and decimals	Write 0.1 as a fraction in its simplest form.	Write 0.35 as a fraction in its simplest form.	If $^n/_{10}$ is how to find 10% of n, express how 5% can be found with one operation using n	Write the fraction that is halfway between 0.36 and 0.37 in its simplest form.
Equivalent fractions and fractions of amounts	Complete the fractions so they are all equivalent to a $^1/_2$ $^1/_2 = {}^2/_?$ $\quad {}^?/_{10}$ $\quad {}^{50}/_?$ $\quad {}^?/_{110}$	Find $^3/_4$ of £2.40	If $^3/_5$ of an amount is £21, how much is the whole amount?	If $^2/_3$ and $^1/_4$ of an amount total £27.50 what is $^1/_6$ of the amount?
Ratio	If toffees to chocolates are mixed 1:3, what fraction are toffees?	Share £24 in the ratio 1:2	Orange juice to lemonade is mixed 1:4. How much lemonade is used in a 2 litre bottle in millilitres?	Nuts to raisins are mixed in a ratio 3:2. What is the total weight of the mix if 750g of nuts are used in kilograms?
Using multiplication facts to solve problems	Which times-table is represented by these letters? n cm cn pm pn tm tn em en nm	$26\ \square \times \square\ 3 = 6072$	If x, y, and z are all positive integers, what is the value of x? $3x + 2y = 31$ $2y + z = 5$	$\begin{array}{\|c\|c\|c\|} \hline \times & \spadesuit & \blacklozenge \\ \hline \blacklozenge & \blacklozenge & \heartsuit \\ \hline \clubsuit & \clubsuit & 6 \\ \hline \end{array}$ Work out which symbol has which value 1 = 2 = 3 = 4 =

Differentiated word problems: Algebra

Topic	one-step	two-step	multi-step	creative multi-step
Using inverse to find the value of n in an equation	$n + 4 = 12$ $n =$	$2n + 8 = 30$ $n =$	$4n + 9 = 89$ $11n =$	$8n + 6 = 5n + 15$ $n =$
Using inverse to find the value from word problems	I start with a number, I add 3 and have 101. What did I start with?	I start with a number, I multiply it by 5 and divide it by 4 to get 15. What did I start with?	I start with a number, I add 11, find 10%, then multiply it by 3 to get 12. What did I start with?	Anna has twice as many marbles as Ben, who has three times as many marbles as Charlie, who has half the marbles of Daisy. Altogether, they have 84 marbles. How many marbles do they each have?
Sequences	Complete: $2, 1, {}^{1}/_{2}, {}^{1}/_{4}, \underline{\ ?\ }$	Complete: $1, 1, 2, 3, 5, 8, \underline{\ ?\ }$	$100, 50, 33.\dot{3}, 25, 20$ What is the 8th number in this sequence?	$-1, 2, 7, 14, 23$ What is the 100th number in this sequence?
Number machines	Find the missing numbers: $1 \to 5$ $2 \to 10$ $3 \to 15$ $4 \to 20$ $5 \to \square$	Find the missing numbers: $1 \to 7$ $2 \to 12$ $3 \to 17$ $4 \to \square$ $5 \to \square$	Complete the sequence that is connected by $3n-1$: $1 \to 2$ $2 \to \square$ $3 \to \square$ $4 \to \square$ $5 \to \square$	 What is the value of n when 121 lines are used?
Rules and formulae	 What is the rule that connects the n number to the resultant number?	If n $1 \to 2$ $2 \to 4$ $3 \to 6$ $4 \to 8$ can be expressed as $2n$, that is $2 \times n$, the nth term is the formula that connects n to the resultant number, find the nth term for: n $1 \to 3$ $2 \to 6$ $3 \to 9$ $4 \to 12$	Use the formula n^2+5 to complete the table: 	Find the nth term for n $1 \to 8$ $2 \to 11$ $3 \to 14$ $4 \to 17$
Formulae with shape and space	If the area of a rectangle is found by base × height, find the area: 	If a square has an area of 64cm^2, what is its perimeter? Area = 64cm^2	If volume = base × height × depth, find the value of x when the volume = 24cm^3: 	Six congruent isosceles triangles make a hexagon. What is its area?

Differentiated word problems: Shape, space and measures

Topic	one-step	two-step	multi-step	creative multi-step
Conversion	Convert 734g to kilograms	How many 125ml glasses of juice can be poured from a one litre carton?	If 5 miles is about 8 kilometres, how far in miles is 12 kilometres?	If 2kg of nuts cost £3, how much would 400g cost?
Angles	What is angle x? x \145°	What is angle x? (circle divided into 6 with x in each section)	A triangle is put in a square: (triangle in square with 50°, x, 40°) What is angle x?	An isosceles triangle is added to a square. What is angle x? (square with triangle on top, x)
Co-ordinates	Write the co-ordinates for A: (grid with rectangle: (1,4), (4,4), A, (4,2))	Write the co-ordinates for M (the mid-point): (2,3) (6,3) M (2,1) (6,1)	Two congruent isosceles triangles are put together. Write the co-ordinates for M (the mid-point): (2,11) (10,11) M (2,3) (10,3)	Write the third co-ordinate for the isosceles triangle: (-4,1) (4,-1)
Area and perimeter	Find the area of the rectangle: 3cm 6cm	Find the perimeter of the rectangle: Area = 30cm² 6cm	What is the value of x? x Area = 52cm² 5cm ←8cm→	Calculate the shaded area: 10cm 8cm ←8cm→
Reflective, rotational symmetry, and translations	(grid with diagonal line and shaded square) Shade in one more square to make a symmetrical shape with the diagonal line being the line of symmetry.	(grid with diagonal line and shaded shape) Shade in three more squares to make a symmetrical shape with the diagonal line being the line of symmetry.	(grid with triangle at 1-3, height 2-3) Translate this shape by (2,1)	Write a three letter word with any of the alphabet capitals that can have 2 as their order of rotational symmetry.
Imperial and metric measurements	1 tonne = 1000kg. How many grams make 1 tonne?	If 1 foot = 12 inches and 1 inch is about 2.5cm, about how many centimetres are there in 1 foot?	If 1 stone is about 6.35kg, convert 8 stone into kilograms.	A 30 miles B 5 miles If 5 miles is about 8 kilometres, how far is A to B in kilometres?

Differentiated word problems: Data handling

Topic	one-step	two-step	multi-step	creative multi-step
Averages	What is the range of 3 and 5 ?	What is the mean of 3 and 5 ?	Write 3 different integers with a mean of 7 and a range of 2 □ □ □	Write 5 integers with a mean of 6, and a mode of 4, a median of 5 and a range of 6 □ □ □ □ □
Carroll and venn diagrams with odd, even prime numbers, factors, multiples and line graphs	Sort the factors of 2 Factors of 2 [tree diagram] odd numbers / even numbers	Place the factors of 10 in the carroll diagram [carroll diagram: numbers — prime / not prime; rows: less than 4, greater than 4]	Organise all the factors of 30 in this venn diagram multiples of 2 — factors of 6 [three-circle venn diagram] prime numbers	What was the average speed of the cyclist's fastest section of the journey, expressed in kilometres per hour (km/hr)? [line graph: Distance (km) vs Time (minutes), 0 to 30, 0 to 60]
Pie charts	30 children voted for which colour highlighter pen they preferred. [pie chart: red, yellow, blue] How many children favoured the yellow highlighter pen?	If $2/3$ of children in a school have school dinners rather than packed lunches, what angle on a pie chart would represent children having school dinners?	Boys to girls in a school are in the ratio 3:2. What angle on a pie chart would represent the boys?	In a wood $1/6$ of the trees are oak, 65% of the remaining trees are birch and the rest are fir trees. If a pie chart is used to show this data, how many degrees represent the fir trees?
Probability	What is the probability of throwing a 3 on a normal die?	What is the probability of rolling an odd number on a normal die?	Explain why there is an equal chance of spinning an odd number on Spinner A and Spinner B: [Spinner A hexagon: 1, 2, 3, 4, 5, 6] [Spinner B square: 1, 2, 3, 4]	What is the probability of spinning an even number on this spinner? [hexagon spinner: 2, 1, 3, 4]
Bar charts	Children voted on their favourite location for a day trip. How many votes are recorded on the bar chart? [bar chart: Amount of votes 0–25, Seaside, Countryside / Location]	A die was rolled and the numbers rolled were recorded. Which number came up $1/4$ of the times? **The amount of numbers rolled on a die** [bar chart: Amount of numbers rolled 0–8, Number on die 1 2 3 4 5 6]	Children voted for the colour of their new sweatshirts. Label the tally and bar chart so that they match the data: [table: blue — ||||| ; red — ||||| |||| ; green — ?] [bar chart: Number of votes, ? ? ? Favourite colour for new sweatshirts]	Six bags of sweets are opened and the sweets are counted. Add a fourth, fifth and sixth bar on the chart below, so the mean of sweets per bag is 4, the modal value is 4 and bag four has most sweets in it: **Number of sweets in a bag** [bar chart: Amount of sweets 0–10, one two three four five six / Bags of sweets]

Differentiated Timed Mental Maths tests

	Topic	Time (secs)	Mental Maths A	Mental Maths B	Mental Maths C	Mental Maths D
1	Number	5	Find the total of 7 and 5.	Find the product of 7 and 5.	Find the difference of 1001 and 998.	What is 60 divided by 24?
2	Place value	5	What is 0.1 as a fraction?	What is 0.07 as a fraction?	What is 0.17 as a fraction?	What is half way between 0.18 and 0.19?
3	Money	5	How much are three pens at 29p each?	How much are four rulers at 35p each?	How much change do I get from £1 if I buy one pen at 29p and one ruler at 35p?	If 3 pens cost 48p, how much are 5 pens?
4	Negative numbers	5	What is the difference between -1 and 4?	It is 5°C in the day. At night time it is 12°C colder, what temperature is it at night?	What comes next in the sequence: 10, 7, 4, 1, ?	What is -5 – -3?
5	Averages	5	What is the mode of 4, 5, 5, 6, ?	What is the median of 3, 4, 5, ?	What is the mean of 10.4 and 3.6 ?	What is the mean of 0.3 and 0.4?
6	Equations	10	Find the value of x when $2x = 9$	Find the value of x when $x + 2y = 21$ $3y=27$	Find the value of x when $4x + 4y = 48$ and $3y = 21$	What is the value of x if $3.6 \div x = 0.036$?
7	Angles	10	One of two angles on a straight line is 45°, what is the other angle?	If the obtuse angles of a parallelogram each measure 120°, what does each acute angle measure?	What is the acute angle between the hands on a clock at two o'clock?	A regular octagon is divided into 8 congruent triangles. What type of triangles are they?
8	Prime numbers, factors and multiples	10	What is the product of the first two prime numbers?	Which odd factor of 10 is also a prime number?	What is the lowest common multiple of 6 and 4?	What is the lowest common multiple of 2, 3 and 4?
9	Shape, reflective and rotational symmetry	10	How many lines of reflective symmetry does a kite have?	Which kind of triangle has three lines of reflective symmetry?	Which kind of triangle has no lines of reflective symmetry?	Which triangle has a rotational symmetry order of 3?
10	Probability	10	On a normal die, what is the probability of rolling a 3?	On a normal die, what is the probability of rolling an odd number?	On a normal die, what is the probability of rolling a number less than 3?	If there is 80% probability of an event occurring, what is this probability expressed as a fraction?
11	Time	10	A bus arrives at a stop at 3.05pm. It is eight minutes late. What time should it have arrived?	How many seconds are in two and a half minutes?	A train leaves Station A at 22:35. It arrives at Station B four hours and forty five minutes later. What time does it arrive?	How many minutes is 660 seconds?
12	Halving and doubling	10	What is double 2.45?	What is half of 3.8?	If 1.75 is half of n, what is $2n$?	What is half of the sum of 4.8 and 4.9?
13	Fractions, decimals and percentages	10	Write 0.6 as a fraction in its simplest form.	Write 34% as a decimal?	Which is worth least? 0.105 11% $^{102}/_{1000}$	What is $^1/_8$ as a percentage?
14	Multiplication	10	What is 40×6?	What is 30×0.9?	What is the product of 0.4×0.1?	What is the volume of a cuboid that measures 2cm by 2cm by 9cm?
15	Place value and fractions	10	What is half way between 0 and 0.1?	What is half way between 0.2 and 0.3 as a fraction?	What is halfway between $^5/_8$ and $^6/_8$?	What is half of $^5/_8$ as its simplest fraction?
16	Fractions	15	What is $^1/_5$ of £10?	What is $^3/_4$ of £12?	If $^3/_4$ of an amount is £21, how much is the amount?	If $^2/_3$ of an amount is £12, what is $^1/_4$ of this amount?
17	Area and perimeter	15	What is the area of a rectangle that measures 4 cm by 5 cm?	If the area of a square is 49 cm², what is its perimeter?	If the area of a triangle is 24 cm² and its base measures 8 cm, what does its height measure?	If a rectangle has an area of 6cm² and a perimeter of 14cm, what are its dimensions?
18	Percentages	15	What is 10% of £9.20?	What is 30% of £3.40?	What is 23% of £4?	If 20% of an amount is 18p, what is the amount?
19	Ratio, Proportion and Pie charts	15	Share £24 in the ratio of 1:3	If 5 miles is about 8 kilometres, how far in miles is 32 kilometres?	What is the ratio of boys to girls in a school, if a pie chart uses 120° to represent the boys?	If A is paid £6 and B is paid £4, what is the ratio of pay for A:B?
20	Conversion	15	What is 2.4 km in metres?	What weight of peanuts are left when 125g of peanuts are eaten from a 1kg packet?	Which is the largest of 3.7 litres, 3750 ml or 371 cl?	What is the range of 95cm and 12m in metres?

Differentiated word problems: Answers

		one-step	two-step	multi-step	creative multi-step
Number	1	$\begin{array}{r} 3\ 4\ 4 \\ +\ 1\ 9\ 8 \\ \hline 5\ 4\ 2 \\ \scriptstyle 1\ \ 1 \end{array}$	4.5	0.615	$6\ 2\ 4 \times 3\ 4$
	2	7.5	8	7	$16.6\dot{6}\%$
	3	72p	£1.39	85p	£2.45
	4	3.7	10.79	31km	1185cl
	5	-18°C	30	30	3cm × 6cm
	6	36	$7 \times 10 = 70$ $7 \times 1 = 7$ $7 \times 0.1 = 0.7$ $7 \times 0.01 = 0.07$	$7 \div 0.01 = 700$ $7 \div 0.1 = 70$ $7 \div 1 = 7$ $7 \div 10 = 0.7$	A smaller product is made when multiplying by a decimal. A larger product is made when dividing by a decimal.
	7	$^1/_{10}$	$^7/_{20}$	$^n/_{20}$	$^{73}/_{200}$
	8	$^2/_4$, $^5/_{10}$, $^{50}/_{100}$, $^{55}/_{110}$	£1.80	£35	£5
	9	$^1/_4$	£8:£16	1600ml	1.25kg
	10	5 times-table	264×23	$x = 9$	1 = ♠, 2 = ♦, 3 = ♣, 4 = ♥

		one-step	two-step	multi-step	creative multi-step
Algebra	1	$n = 8$	$n = 11$	$n = 220$	$n=3$
	2	$n = 98$	$n = 12$	$n = 29$	Anna = 42, Ben = 21, Charlie = 7, Daisy = 14
	3	$^1/_8$	13	12.5	9998
	4	25	$4 \rightarrow 22$ $5 \rightarrow 27$	$2 \rightarrow 5$ $3 \rightarrow 8$ $4 \rightarrow 11$ $5 \rightarrow 14$	30
	5	×2	$3n$	<table><tr><td>1</td><td>2</td><td>3</td><td>7</td><td>8</td><td>10</td></tr><tr><td>6</td><td>9</td><td>14</td><td>54</td><td>69</td><td>105</td></tr></table>	$3n + 5$
	6	28cm²	32cm	$x = 4cm$	72cm²

		one-step	two-step	multi-step	creative multi-step
Shape, space and measures	1	0.734kg	8	7.5 miles	60p
	2	35°	72°	10°	225°
	3	(1,2)	(4,2)	(6,7)	(-4, -3)
	4	18cm²	22cm	8cm	32cm²
	5				Any three letter word can be made from HNIOSXZ eg.: SIX or HIS
	6	1000000g	30cm	50.8kg	56km

		one-step	two-step	multi-step	creative multi-step
Data handling	1	2	4	6, 7, 8	4, 4, 5, 7, 10
	2	Factors of 2 — odd numbers: 1; even numbers: 2	<table><tr><td>2</td><td>1</td></tr><tr><td>5</td><td>10</td></tr></table>		50km/hr
	3	15	240°	216°	105°
	4	$^1/_6$	$^1/_2$	$^3/_6 = ^2/_4$ or both have $^1/_2$ odd numbers	$^2/_6 = ^1/_3$
	5	40	5	y-axis = 3, 6, 9, 12 x-axis = blue, green, red	bag four = 7 sweets bag five = 4 sweets bag six = 4 sweets

Differentiated Timed Mental Maths tests: Answers

	Mental Maths – A	Mental Maths – B	Mental Maths – C	Mental Maths – D
1	12	35	3	2.5
2	$^1/_{10}$	$^7/_{100}$	$^{17}/_{100}$	0.185
3	87p	£1.40	36p	80p
4	5	-7°C	-2	-2
5	5	4	7	0.35
6	4.5	$x = 3$	$x = 5$	100
7	135º	60º	60º	Isosceles
8	6	5	12	12
9	One	Equilateral	Scalene or right-angled scalene	Equilateral
10	$^1/_6$	$^1/_2$	$^1/_3$	$^4/_5$
11	2.57pm	150 seconds	3.20am	11
12	4.9	1.9	7	4.85
13	$^3/_5$	0.34	$^{102}/_{1000}$	12.5%
14	240	27	0.04	36cm³
15	0.05	$^{25}/_{100}$ or $^1/_4$	$^{11}/_{16}$	$^5/_{16}$
16	£2	£9	£28	£4.50
17	20cm²	28cm	6cm	1cm × 6cm
18	92p	£1.02	92p	90p
19	£6:£18	20 miles	1:2	3:2
20	2,400m	875g	3,750ml	11.05m

Scholarship questions

Scholarship questions involve novel challenges that require the creative application to known concepts. Think what you know about each topic and what you need to do in order to solve the problem.

Number

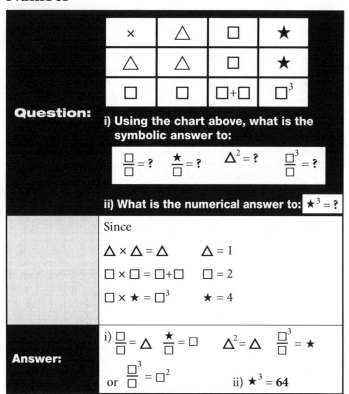

Question:

i) Using the chart above, what is the symbolic answer to:

$$\frac{\square}{\square} = ? \qquad \frac{\star}{\square} = ? \qquad \triangle^2 = ? \qquad \frac{\square^3}{\square} = ?$$

ii) What is the numerical answer to: $\star^3 = ?$

Since

$$\triangle \times \triangle = \triangle \qquad \triangle = 1$$

$$\square \times \square = \square + \square \qquad \square = 2$$

$$\square \times \star = \square^3 \qquad \star = 4$$

Answer:

i) $\dfrac{\square}{\square} = \triangle \quad \dfrac{\star}{\square} = \square \quad \triangle^2 = \triangle \quad \dfrac{\square^3}{\square} = \star$

or $\dfrac{\square^3}{\square} = \square^2$

ii) $\star^3 = 64$

Question:

If cog-wheel A goes round 48 times per hour, how many times does cog-wheel B and cog-wheel C go round in one hour?

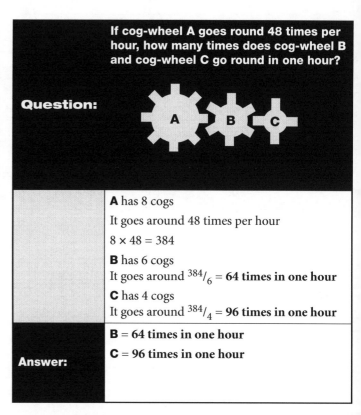

A has 8 cogs

It goes around 48 times per hour

$8 \times 48 = 384$

B has 6 cogs

It goes around $^{384}/_6 =$ **64 times in one hour**

C has 4 cogs

It goes around $^{384}/_4 =$ **96 times in one hour**

Answer:

B = 64 times in one hour

C = 96 times in one hour

Algebra

Question:

Each triangle represents two sums (using integers) acting on each number in a set order. What are the sums?

1 $\triangle$ $\triangle$ 1

2 $\triangle$ $\triangle$ 1.25

3 $\triangle$ $\triangle$ 1.5

4 $\triangle$ $\triangle$ 1.75

5 $\triangle$ $\triangle$ 2

1 ➝ 1
2 ➝ 1.25
3 ➝ 1.5
4 ➝ 1.75
5 ➝ 2

Notice that the link between the initial number (n) and the final number is: $\dfrac{n + 3}{4}$

So, know that addition and division are involved. Try different low integers with adding and dividing.

$\triangle$ = add 1 then divide by 2; the process is repeated...

Answer:

So, $1 \xrightarrow{+1} 2 \xrightarrow{\div 2} 1 \xrightarrow{+1} 2 \xrightarrow{\div 2} 1$
$2 \rightarrow 3 \rightarrow 1.5 \rightarrow 2.5 \rightarrow 1.25$
$3 \rightarrow 4 \rightarrow 2 \rightarrow 3 \rightarrow 1.5$
$4 \rightarrow 5 \rightarrow 2.5 \rightarrow 3.5 \rightarrow 1.75$
$5 \rightarrow 6 \rightarrow 3 \rightarrow 4 \rightarrow 2$

Question:

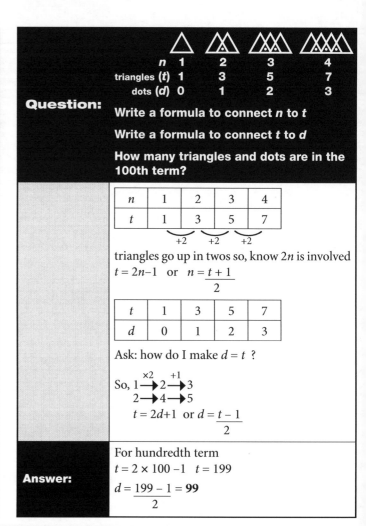

n	1	2	3	4
triangles (t)	1	3	5	7
dots (d)	0	1	2	3

Write a formula to connect n to t

Write a formula to connect t to d

How many triangles and dots are in the 100th term?

n	1	2	3	4
t	1	3	5	7

+2   +2   +2

triangles go up in twos so, know $2n$ is involved

$t = 2n-1$ or $n = \dfrac{t + 1}{2}$

t	1	3	5	7
d	0	1	2	3

Ask: how do I make $d = t$?

So, $1 \xrightarrow{\times 2} 2 \xrightarrow{+1} 3$
$2 \rightarrow 4 \rightarrow 5$

$t = 2d+1$ or $d = \dfrac{t - 1}{2}$

Answer:

For hundredth term

$t = 2 \times 100 - 1 \quad t = 199$

$d = \dfrac{199 - 1}{2} = 99$

Shape, space and measures

Question: The perimeter of the large rhombus is 20cm. The perimeter of each small black rhombus is 8cm.

What is the area of the white section?

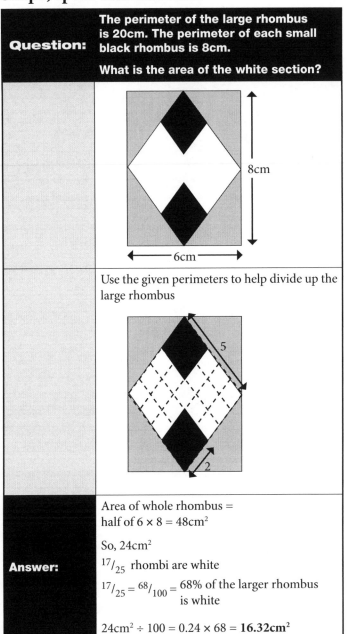

Use the given perimeters to help divide up the large rhombus

Answer:

Area of whole rhombus =
half of 6 × 8 = 48cm²

So, 24cm²

$^{17}/_{25}$ rhombi are white

$^{17}/_{25} = {}^{68}/_{100} = 68\%$ of the larger rhombus is white

24cm² ÷ 100 = 0.24 × 68 = **16.32cm²**

Question: Find the value of angle x

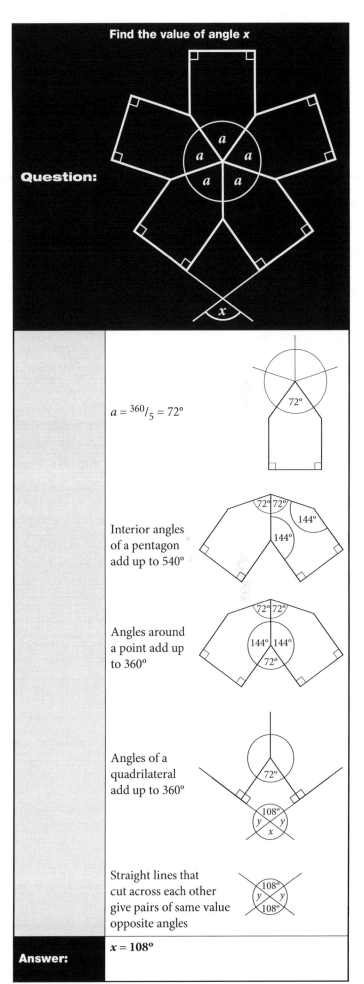

$a = {}^{360}/_5 = 72°$

Interior angles of a pentagon add up to 540°

Angles around a point add up to 360°

Angles of a quadrilateral add up to 360°

Straight lines that cut across each other give pairs of same value opposite angles

Answer: $x = 108°$

Data handling

Question:	Complete the labelling for this sorting tree when X is written with 90° angles between lines and O is written as a circle:

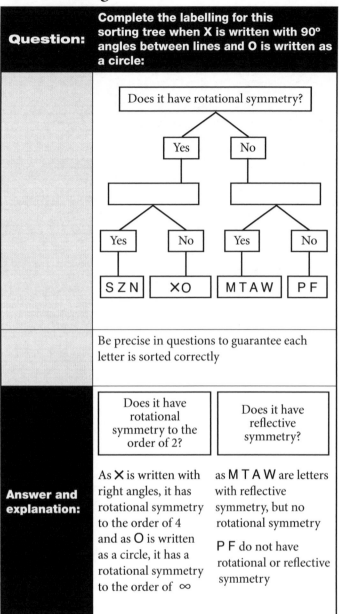

Be precise in questions to guarantee each letter is sorted correctly

Answer and explanation:	Does it have rotational symmetry to the order of 2?

As **X** is written with right angles, it has rotational symmetry to the order of 4 and as **O** is written as a circle, it has a rotational symmetry to the order of ∞

Does it have reflective symmetry?

as **M T A W** are letters with reflective symmetry, but no rotational symmetry

P F do not have rotational or reflective symmetry

Question:	Two identical spinners are spun and the two numbers added to make a total. • There is a probability of 1 that the totals are even • There is a probability of 1 that the totals are 6 or less • There is 9 times more probability of getting a total of 2 than a total of 6 • There is 1.5 times more probability of getting a total of 2 than a total of 4 **Write in the four numbers on each spinner**

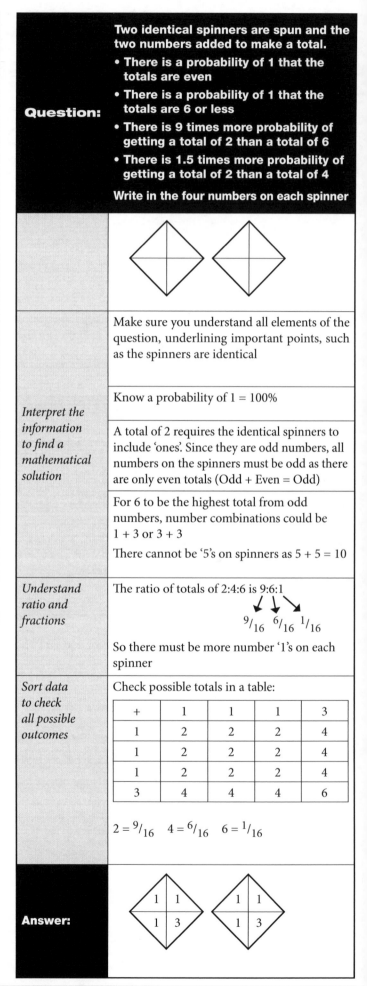

Interpret the information to find a mathematical solution	Make sure you understand all elements of the question, underlining important points, such as the spinners are identical
	Know a probability of 1 = 100%
	A total of 2 requires the identical spinners to include 'ones'. Since they are odd numbers, all numbers on the spinners must be odd as there are only even totals (Odd + Even = Odd)
	For 6 to be the highest total from odd numbers, number combinations could be $1 + 3$ or $3 + 3$ There cannot be '5's on spinners as $5 + 5 = 10$
Understand ratio and fractions	The ratio of totals of 2:4:6 is 9:6:1 $\frac{9}{16}$ $\frac{6}{16}$ $\frac{1}{16}$ So there must be more number '1's on each spinner
Sort data to check all possible outcomes	Check possible totals in a table:

+	1	1	1	3
1	2	2	2	4
1	2	2	2	4
1	2	2	2	4
3	4	4	4	6

$2 = \frac{9}{16}$ $4 = \frac{6}{16}$ $6 = \frac{1}{16}$

Answer:	

MATHEMATICS – TEST PAPER ONE

Time: 45 minutes – No calculator allowed

1) $45 + 17 + 2.9 =$

1 mark

2) If £6.30 ÷ 7 = 90p
   What is £6.30 ÷ 70?

1 mark

3) What is the range of 3 and 101?

1 mark

4) If 4 pens cost 88p, how much would 14 pens cost?

1 mark

5) Put these values in order (smallest first):

   a) $^4/_5$ 0.75 $^7/_{10}$ 85%

2 marks

   b) 1.1   1.01   1.001   1.11

6) Write five numbers with a mean of 6, a median of 7, a mode of 9 and a range of 8:

1 mark

☐ ☐ ☐ ☐ ☐

7) Draw crosses to the drawn circles to fit each ratio:

2 marks

 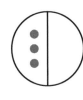 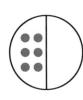

     2:1   3:2   3:2   1:1

8) Find the value of n for each sum:

4 marks

   a) $n + 3 = 10$ $n =$

   b) $4n + 6 = 90$ $n =$

   c) $^n/_4 = 7$ $n =$

   d) $^n/_{40} = 10$ $n =$

9) Write $^3/_8$ as a decimal and mark, with an arrow, where it would go on the line:

1 mark

|⎸|⎸|⎸|⎸|⎸|⎸|⎸|⎸|⎸|⎸|

0   1

10) a) What is 30% of £9?

   b) What is 18% of £9?

   2 marks

11) a) Convert 92cm to metres

   b) Convert 106km to centimetres

   2 marks

12) Calculate the perimeter of the following quadrilaterals:

   3 marks

| Area A = 21cm² | | Area B = 14cm² | 3.5cm | | Area C = 32cm² | a |

Area A = 21cm²

7cm

Area B = 14cm²   3.5cm

Area C = 32cm² a

2a

perimeter A =   perimeter B =   perimeter C =

13) If 3 pizzas and 4 colas cost £6.50, and 5 colas cost £2.50, how much would 2 pizzas and 3 colas cost?

   1 mark

14) A pizza contains 360 calories. It is cut into 8 slices and Anne eats 5 slices.

   How many calories has she consumed?

   1 mark

15) Plot the co-ordinates below and write the formulae to express the relationship between x and y.

   Co-ordinates: (-2, -4), (-1, -2), (0, 0), (1, 2), (2, 4)

   2 marks

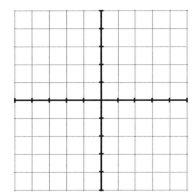

$x =$

$y =$

16) Find each angle:

   2 marks

a) 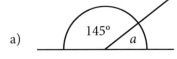   145° a $a =$

b) 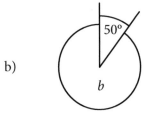   50° b $b =$

17) An isosceles triangle is put in a square. Find angles *x* and *y*.

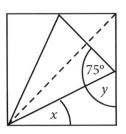

2 marks

  a) *x* =

  b) *y* =

18)

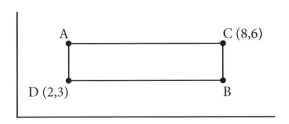

2 marks

  A = (,)

  B = (,)

19) $\frac{1}{5}$ of the biscuits are eaten and 28 are left. How many biscuits were there originally?

1 mark

20) a) $\frac{2}{3} + \frac{1}{6} =$

  b) $\frac{1}{2} - \frac{1}{3} =$

2 marks

21) Three films are shown at a cinema, each lasting the same time, with a ten minute interval between each. If the first film begins at 14:05 and the last film ends at 19:40. What time does the second film start?

1 mark

22) A cyclist rides from *Ace Town* to *Busy Town* as shown by the line graph:

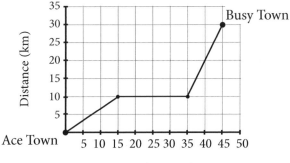

3 marks

  a) How long does the cyclist rest for?

  b) Is the cyclist faster before or after the rest break?

  c) If the cyclist did not stop, but continued at the first pace, how long would it take the cyclist to cycle from *Ace Town* to *Busy Town*?

23) A pie chart is divided to show the amount of tree types in a park. State the angle that each tree type will take on the pie chart.

2 marks

Tree type	Number	Angle on pie chart
Oak	90	
Pine	45	
Silver Birch	30	
Beech	15	

24) A 1 Litre bottle of water is poured into glasses that hold 25cl. How many glasses can filled?

1 mark

25)   −2   −1   3   5   11

    a) Write down two of the above numbers with a range of 5:

    b) Write down two of the above numbers that add to make 2:

    c) Write down two of the above numbers that add to make −3:

3 marks

26) What is the volume of these shapes?

               A   B

2 marks

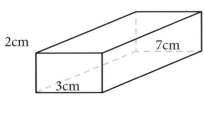
2cm   7cm   3cm

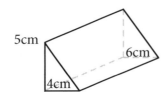
5cm   6cm   4cm

    shape A =   shape B =

27) A 12km journey takes 45 minutes. What is the speed (per hour)?

1 mark

28) A shirt cost £36. It is reduced by 10%. What does it cost now?

1 mark

29) A shirt now costs £49 after it is reduced by 30%. What did it originally cost?

1 mark

30) Purple paint contains red to blue paint in the ratio 3:2. How much blue paint is needed to go with 15cl of red paint?

1 mark

Total: _____
50

ANSWERS: MATHEMATICS TEST PAPER ONE

1) **64.9**

2) **9p**

3) **98**

4) **£3.08**

5) a) $^7/_{10}$, **0.75**, $^4/_5$, **85%**

   b) **1.001, 1.01, 1.1, 1.11**

6) **1, 4, 7, 9, 9**

7)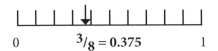

8) a) $n = 7$ b) $n = 21$ c) $n = 28$ d) $n = 400$

9)

$^3/_8 = 0.375$

10) a) **£2.70**   b) **£1.62**

11) a) **0.92m**   b) **10,600,000cm**

12) A = **20cm**, B = **15cm**, C = **24cm**

13) **£4.50**

14) **225 calories**

15)

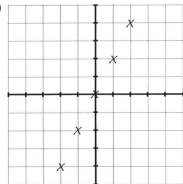

$x = y/_2$
$y = 2x$

16) a) $a = 35°$ b) $b = 310°$

17) a) $x = 30°$ b) $y = 60°$

18) A = **(2,6)**, B = **(8,3)**

19) **35**

20) a) $^5/_6$ b) $^1/_6$

21) **16:00**

22) a) **20 minutes**   b) **faster after the rest break**   c) **45 minutes**

23) **180°, 90°, 60°, 30°**

24) **4 glasses**

25) a) **–2, 3**   b) **–1, 3**   c) **–2, –1**

26) A = **42cm³**, B = **60cm³**

27) **16km/hr**

28) **£32.40**

29) **£70**

30) **10cl**

MATHEMATICS – TEST PAPER TWO

Time: 45 minutes – No calculator allowed

1) Complete the sequences:

    a) 1, 2, 4, 7, _____

    b) 11, 8, 5, 2, _____

    c) 1, 4, 9, 16, _____

    d) 1, 8, 27, 64, _____

☐ 4 marks

2) Write in the missing numbers to make these sums correct:

    a)
```
    ☐ 3
  +  4 ☐
  ───────
    9 7
```

    b)
```
    ☐ 5
  +  8 ☐
  ───────
  1 5 1
```

☐ 2 marks

3) Find the value of x for each sum:

    a) $x - 9 = 21$ $x =$

    b) $(x + 5) \times 7 = 63$ $x =$

    c) $x \div 10 = 0.41$ $x =$

    d) $10x = 0.69$ $x =$

☐ 4 marks

4) Work out the total area of these four congruent triangles:

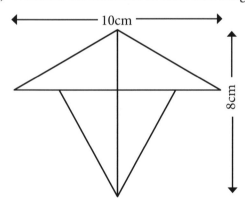

☐ 2 marks

5) Work out the area of this shape:

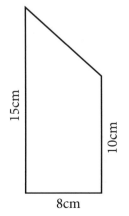

☐ 1 mark

6) Bella has three times as much money as Jake. Jake has two times as much money as Lucy.
Altogether they have £54. How much does each person have?

1 mark

Bella _____   Jake _____   Lucy _____

7) A shirt costing £78 is reduced by 15%. What does it cost now?

1 mark

8) What percentage of this shape is shaded?

2 marks

9) Label the bars on this bar chart with the children's names:

2 marks

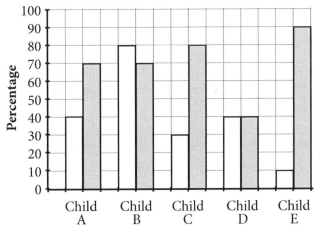

☐ English score

▨ Maths score

Jo's mean score for both tests was 55%. Lisa had the greatest range of results.
Tring had twice the score for English than Annie. Samuel had the same score for Maths and English.

10) Use these signs between the values: > < =

5 marks

a) $^1/_5$ $^1/_6$

b) $^7/_{11}$ 0.69

c) 27%   0.275

d) 1.01   101%

e) −3   −4

11) Write in the numbers on this spinner so that:
there is an even chance of getting an odd number;
the mode number is 4;
there is a 1/6 chance of getting a 2; and
there is zero chance of getting a number greater than 5.

1 mark

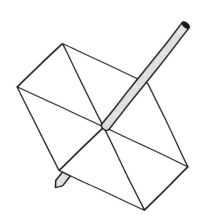

12) Complete the drawing so that it has reflective symmetry:

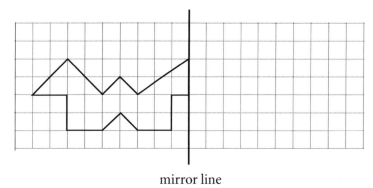

mirror line

13) Write down the co-ordinates of A on this parallelogram:

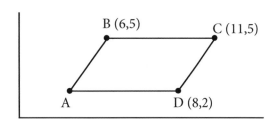

A = (,   )

14) If 5 rulers cost £1.10, what is the change from £5 for 8 rulers?

1 mark

15) Draw a pentagon that has one pair of parallel lines, three right angles and one line of reflective symmetry:

1 mark

16) Isosceles triangles are placed on a straight line. Work out the marked angles:

3 marks

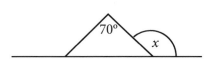 x =

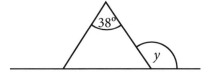 y =

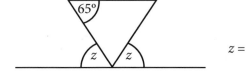 z =

17) A dress costs £36 or $60. If a top costs $135, how much is this in pounds sterling?

1 mark

18) Jan leaves Apple Town at 08:10 and arrives in Banana Town at 08:55. What speed is she travelling?

1 mark

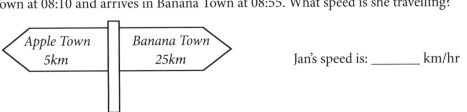

Jan's speed is: _____ km/hr

19) It's 16:15. Josh has some spare time. He spends half of it watching TV. He then spends half of the remaining time cooking. He then spends half of the remaining time reading. He has ten minutes to go out. What time does he go out?

1 mark

20) Calculate the change from £10 having purchased 14 pencils at 59p each.

1 mark

21) Circle the shape(s) that have rotational symmetry:

1 mark

a)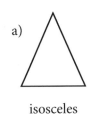

isosceles
triangle

b)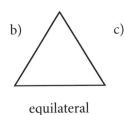

equilateral
triangle

c)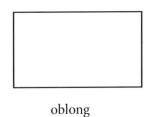

oblong

d)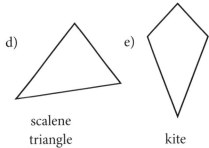

scalene
triangle

e)

kite

22) Complete this venn diagram:

1 mark

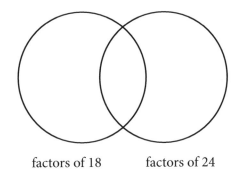

factors of 18   factors of 24

23) A regular pentagon is divided into triangles. What is angle x ?

1 mark

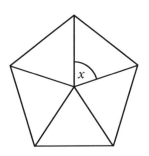

$x =$

24) The tortoise travels at a constant speed of 30m/h.
   The hare travels at 120m/h but stops for a 30 minute rest every 15 minutes.

   a) Who wins the 45 metre race?

   b) What is the difference between the competitor's finishing times?

   c) Plot the two races.

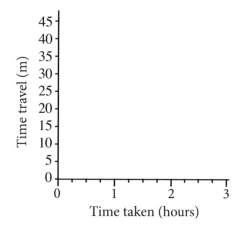

25) Tick the net of the cube that is of the cube shown:

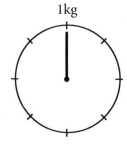 a) 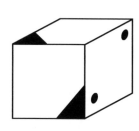 b) 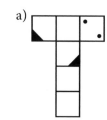 c)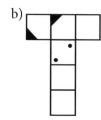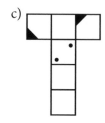

26) Work out the value of x when the perimeter of the hexagon is 53cm

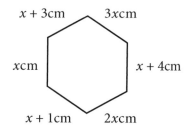

   $x =$ _____ cm

27) Mark 125g with an arrow on each scale:

1kg

0   1kg

28) Who won the running race?

Name	Time (secs)
Alice	21.03
Beth	19.13
Connor	19.15
Daniel	18.95

1 mark

29) Who won the long jump?

Name	Distance (m)
Alice	3.1
Beth	4.9
Connor	4.92
Daniel	4.37

1 mark

30) £11.12 is divided in the ratio 5:3. How much is each share worth?

1 mark

Total: ——— / 50

ANSWERS: MATHEMATICS TEST PAPER TWO

1) a) **11** b) **–1** c) **25** d) **125**

2) a)
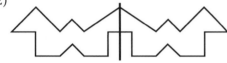
b)

3) a) **30** b) **4** c) **4.1** d) **0.069**

4) **30cm²**

5) **100cm²**

6) **Bella = £36, Jake = £12, Lucy = £6**

7) **£66.30**

8) **52%**

9) **A= Annie, B = Tring, C = Jo, D = Samuel, E = Lisa**

10) a) **>** b) **<** c) **<** d) **=** e) **>**

11) **1, 2, 3, 4, 4, 5**

12)
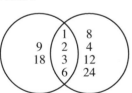

13) **A = (3, 2)**

14) **£3.24**

15) Such as:

16) a) $x = 125°$ b) $y = 109°$ c) $z = 65°$

17) **£81**

18) **40km/hr**

19) **17:35**

20) **£1.74**

21) **b** and **c**

22)
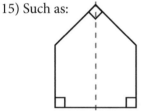

23) $x = 72°$

24) a) **hare** b) **37 minutes and 30 seconds (or 37.5 minutes)**

c)
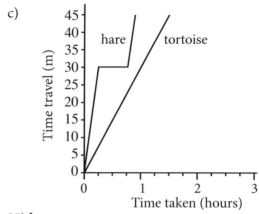

25) **b**

26) $x = 5cm$

27)
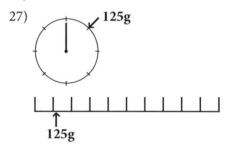

28) **Daniel**

29) **Connor**

30) **£6.95 : £4.17**

MATHEMATICS – TEST PAPER THREE

Time: 45 minutes – No calculator allowed

1) Complete the table:

2 marks

x	a)	b)	c)
d)	2.6	6.5	130
3	6	15	e)

2) Work out the product of:

20.9 and 1.6

1 mark

3) Find the value of x for each sum:

4 marks

   a) $100x = 30.5$ $x =$

   b) $1000x = 4$ $x =$

   c) $x \div 10 = 0.875$ $x =$

   d) $(x + 9) \times 4 = 54$ $x =$

4) Write 3 different numbers with a mean of 6, a range of 10, and a median of 6:

1 mark

5) Circle the pattern that shows the 90° clockwise rotation of this original pattern:

1 mark

6) Work out the total volume of these four blocks which have the same dimensions:

2 marks

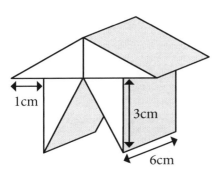

1cm   3cm   6cm

7) Work out the shaded area of this square:

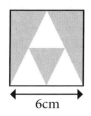

6cm

□ 1 mark

8) Shade in 75% of this shape:

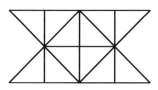

□ 1 mark

9) If 3 apples and 2 bananas cost £1.70, and 4 apples and 2 bananas cost £2.00, how much is:

   a) an apple _____

   b) a banana _____

□ 2 marks

10) In a class, boys to girls carries a ratio of 4:3. If there are 16 boys, how many children are there in the class?

□ 1 mark

11) Work out the co-ordinates for Point A on this isosceles triangle:

□ 1 mark

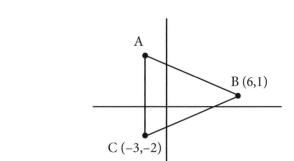

   A = (,)

12) Write the fraction of the shaded area of this shape in its simplest form:

□ 1 mark

13) Use any 3 of these cards to make:

□ 3 marks

   a) The fraction worth least

   b) The proper fraction worth most

   c) Now, use any 4 cards to make a fraction that is equivalent to $^1/_3$

14) What is the reflex angle made by the two hands of a clock at these times?

    a) 03:00

    b) 20:00

    c) 11:00

    d) 22:00

4 marks

15) If it takes 8 people 20 minutes to clean a large shop, how long will it take for 10 people to clean this shop?

1 mark

16) There are n people in House A, $n - 1$ people in House B and $n + 2$ people in House C. Using n, how many people are there altogether?

1 mark

17) Write the values that are half way between the following:

    a) 0.1   _____   1.1

    b) –4   _____   3

    c) $1/5$ _____ $2/5$

    d) 3.6   _____   3.7

4 marks

18) What is the probability of scoring 4 on this spinner?

1 mark

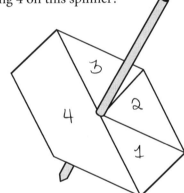

19) Work out the area and perimeter of this shape, made up of overlapping squares:

2 marks

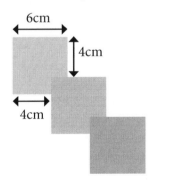

    area =

    perimeter =

20) Oliver jogs between points A and B on a map (with a scale 1:50,000) in 10 minutes. What is his speed?

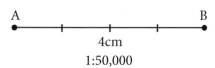

A   B

4cm

1:50,000

_____ km/hr

1 mark

21) What percentage is 48cm out of 4m?

1 mark

22) Use > < = between each pair of values:

   a) 0.75 litre _____ 75cl

   b) 1/3 _____ 3/10

   c) 0.05km _____ 500m

   d) 5/8 _____ 0.7

4 marks

23) This pie chart shows the colour of children's eyes in a school.
If 75 children have blue eyes, how many have brown eyes?

1 mark

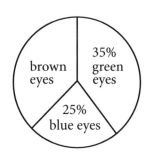

24) Books cost £1.25 and sell for £2.99. A class sells 24 of them, how much profit do they make?

1 mark

25) Place these numbers (1, 2, 3, 4, 5) in the carroll diagram:

2 marks

	Is a square number	Is a prime number
Is even		
Is odd		

26) Each shape has a value:

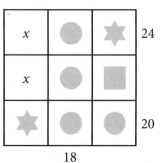

$x \; = \;$

1 mark

27) A man gives half his money to charity. He gives half of the rest to his best friend.
He spends one third of the rest on a car. He has £12,000 left. How much did he start with?

1 mark

28) Write in each box below the name of one of these shapes (parallelogram, kite, trapezium, square)
so that the diagram reads correctly:

2 marks

Has two pairs of parallel sides

Yes   No

Has four right angles   Has one pair of parallel sides

Yes   No   Yes   No

[ ]   [ ]   [ ]   [ ]

29) A minibus can hold 12 people. 54 people are going on a trip. How many minibuses are needed?

1 mark

30) There are 42 eggs. How many dozen egg boxes can be filled?

1 mark

Total: ——————
                50

ANSWERS: MATHEMATICS TEST PAPER THREE

1) a) **2** b) **5** c) **100** d) **1.3** e) **300**

2) **33.44**

3) a) $x = 0.305$ b) $x = 0.004$ c) $x = 8.75$ d) $x = 4.5$

4)

5)

6) **72cm³**

7) **22.5cm²**

8)

9) **Apple = 30p, Banana = 40p**

10) **28 children**

11) **A = (–3, 4)**

12) $^2/_5$

13) a) $^1/_{65}$ b) $^6/_{12}$ c) $^{12}/_{36}$

14) a) **270°** b) **240°** c) **330°** d) **300°**

15) **16 minutes**

16) $3n+1$

17) a) **0.6** b) **–0.5** c) **0.3 or $^3/_{10}$** d) **3.65**

18) $^1/_2$

19) **Area = 100cm², Perimeter = 56cm**

20) **12km/hr**

21) **12%**

22) a) **=** b) **>** c) **<** d) **<**

23) **120**

24) **£41.76**

25)

4	2
1	3 and 5

26) $x = 10$

27) **£72,000**

28) | Square | Parallelogram | Trapezium | Kite |

29) **5**

30) **3**